# TAXMAN TACTICS

# TAXMAN TACTICS
## HOW TO PLAY BY THE RULES - AND WIN!

## STEPHEN COURTNEY

First published in Great Britain in 1990
by Sidgwick & Jackson Ltd
a division of Pan Macmillan Publishers Ltd
18–21 Cavaye Place London SW10 9PG

Reprinted 1992

ISBN 0 283 06031 X

Typset by Pan Macmillan Production Ltd
Printed and bound in Great Britain by
Billing and Sons Limited, Worcester.

# ACKNOWLEDGEMENTS

I am greatly indebted to all those Inspectors of Taxes and other officers of the Inland Revenue with whom I have had many and varied dealings over the years and who have unwittingly provided much of the material for this book. Some Inspectors of Taxes are warm and friendly, others are positively unpleasant, but they all have a job to do; they just approach it differently and it is these differences which make life interesting. Unfortunately they must all remain anonymous, however tempting it may be to expose or praise them.

Grateful thanks are also due to clients (large and small) who have been the subjects (or victims) of the taxman's attentions, because it is largely the trials and tribulations I have suffered on their behalf that form the basis of this book.

Finally, special thanks must be given to my secretary Linda for her skill and patience in typing and amending endless drafts in most difficult circumstances.

S.C.

# CONTENTS

# INTRODUCTION

It is fair to say that most of the population will be concerned with the taxman at some time or another. Sooner or later he will want to communicate with you about your tax affairs – if only to send you a tax return. But not everybody is sent a tax return; the taxman does not bother if you are taxed under PAYE and have no other income. However, you may decide that you should contact him: you might want to make sure that your PAYE deductions are right and that you have received your proper allowances. You may get married, or take out a mortgage to buy a house, and these things affect the tax you pay. If your affairs are more complicated you will get letters from the Inland Revenue and demands to pay tax. You will be very lucky to escape their attention for very long.

People have different attitudes to the taxman; some are absolutely and irrationally terrified, regarding the taxman as some kind of Gestapo to be obeyed without question. At the other extreme there are those foolish beings (usually with dangerously little knowledge) who regard the taxman as some kind of simple punter who is easily conned. People in both categories exist in quite large numbers and it is the latter group who are the most misguided. At least the timid and terrified taxpayer is more likely to be treated fairly reasonably by the taxman – officers of the Inland Revenue generally do try to do their public duty and although they may not get it right all the time, at least they will not usually deliberately do the taxpayer down. On the other hand the taxpayer who sets out to pull the wool over the taxman's eyes will almost certainly do so by lies, half truths or deception – and this is not unnaturally going to cause the taxman to become extremely hostile. It will become clear that a hostile taxman is undoubtedly something to be avoided. However most taxpayers are ordinary people earning an honest living who regard tax as a necessary evil and who live in hope that the taxman is calculating their tax correctly because they don't understand it at all. Some take professional advice but accountants are expensive and this puts many people off – although accountants will nearly always say that they will save you more tax than they will charge in fees. This may or may not be true and the whole subject of whether you should have an accountant acting on your behalf is considered in Chapter 3.

The essential theme of this book is to inform. Nobody who has had anything to do with tax can get anywhere unless they understand how the system works and have an idea of the rules which are involved. It is a subject of immense complexity and one in which rumours and bar-room gossip play a disproportionate and dangerous part. I hope to dispel some of the many mysteries which exist in taxation and to enable the ordinary taxpayer who becomes concerned with the taxman to have at least a reasonable idea of how to approach him without too much apprehension or anxiety. But it is just as important to know how to avoid trouble and I concentrate heavily on the taxman's powers to cause you a lot of aggravation if you do not deal with your tax affairs properly or promptly. Even minor irregularities can put you in trouble and you need to know what the taxman can do (and what he cannot do), as well as what arguments you can use to avoid or minimize your difficulties. For those who are tempted to think that the Inland Revenue is a push-over, a few facts of life about taxation may be useful, if only as a preventative measure. For the middle ground of ordinary people who get caught up unwittingly with the Inland Revenue I hope to explain enough of the system so that they do not get taken advantage of by aggressive Inspectors of Taxes who are not of the warm and friendly type.

This is not a technical book – it will not tell you how to save tax directly – but what it will do is help to even the balance when you find yourself in correspondence (or worse at an interview) with the taxman. He is an expert – you are not. He wants some of your money and he gets it by saying you should pay some tax. He may be taking a narrow view on a technical point which may not be justified – but you are not able to tell whether he is right or wrong. The complexity of the subject means that even Inspectors of Taxes make innocent errors over technical points, but they still put their views forward firmly and sincerely.

To avoid any possible doubt I would emphasize that nowhere in this book is it suggested that anything should be improperly concealed from the Inland Revenue nor that they should be deceived in any way. You do not beat the taxman by cheating – indeed it is a clear admission that you cannot achieve your objective by proper means and have to resort to fraud. No reputable professional person will countenance fraudulent behaviour and he would be mad to do so – he runs the risk of being charged with criminal conspiracy and the loss of his livelihood. I have heard of selfless devotion to one's clients but that is going too far. What client is worth such a sacrifice – and what client would think well of an adviser who acted in such a manner?

A strange morality seems to exist when it comes to tax. Some of the most upright citizens who are scrupulous in all their financial affairs suddenly find a new morality when dealing with the taxman, and will fiddle their taxes (in a small way of course) without compunction. It is very strange. This is the problem which faces the Inland Revenue and which shapes their entire approach. They try hard to get people to take their obligations seriously but without a great deal of success. Stiff penalties are not enough as a deterrent because there is no doubt that tax penalties can already be really swingeing.What is required is a shift in public opinion. When Lester Piggott was sentenced to prison for tax fraud he received a great deal of public sympathy. If he had defrauded an insurance company or robbed a train he would have received no sympathy at all – he would have been branded as dishonest and a thief. As it is, it seems that being convicted and even imprisoned for tax offences involves very little stigma.

Let there be no doubt. Tax evasion is a crime. You can hedge it around as much as you like but it is still a crime. It can take many forms and therefore may comprise many types of offence but even at its simplest it is still a crime. For a start there is the ancient common law offence of cheating Her Majesty's Revenue - which includes any omission or concealment of a pecuniary nature to the prejudice of the Crown. The fact that it is an ancient offence should be give anybody any comfort; this was the charge laid against Lester Piggott who received a prison sentence as a result, and there are many other examples which did not hit the headlines.

Nevertheless it is appropriate to recall the words of Lord Clyde in 1929:

No man in this country is under the smallest obligation, moral or other, so to arrange his legal relations to his business or to his property as to enable the Inland Revenue to put the largest shovel into his stores. The Inland Revenue is not slow – and quite rightly – to take every advantage which is open to it under the taxing statutes for the purpose of depleting the taxpayer's pocket. And the taxpayer is in like manner, entitled to be as astute to prevent, as far as he honestly can, the depletion of his means by the Revenue.

This is really a statement of principle about the relationship between the taxpayer and the Inland Revenue. To the professional taxman and to the professional tax adviser it can be regarded as a game; but this is sometimes thought by taxpayers to be a trivialisation – after all it is he who is footing the bill. Nevertheless it is in many respects a game but as long as you play by the rules you should be safe – providing the taxman is playing by the rules as well.

I hope that by explaining some of the everyday problems which arise with the Inland Revenue and by giving practical guidance on the tactics to be employed, the ordinary taxpayer without (or indeed even with) professional advice, will be better able to ward off the taxman should he find himself in difficulty – and perhaps more importantly, better able to stay out of trouble in the first place.

If this book goes some way towards a greater appreciation of, and adherence to, the rules by both sides it will have served a purpose.

# Chapter One

# THE INLAND REVENUE

## Offices and Procedures

# THE INLAND REVENUE

*The Office Network*

The Inland Revenue is divided into various parts and you will mainly be concerned with the tax office for your district. Each district has its own specified area and is responsible for ensuring that all taxpayers in that district are properly assessed to tax. Each district has a District Inspector who is the Chief; there will be a number of Inspectors of Taxes of various levels of seniority, one of whom will be the Deputy District Inspector; under them there will be Tax Officers of different grades. You will probably be mainly concerned with a higher grade tax officer and with the Inspector of Taxes who has overall responsibility for your affairs. He is an important person because it will be he who makes most of the decisions about how and when you will be taxed. You will correspond with him about your business accounts and negotiate the level of profit chargeable as well as the deductions you feel should be allowed. The Collector of Taxes is a completely separate office which deals with the collection of tax once it has been assessed by the Inspector. There is little communication between the tax office and the Collector of Taxes so do not be surprised if you receive conflicting information from each one.

Much of this book is concerned with how to deal with the ordinary tax office but you should be aware of some other parts of the Inland Revenue organisation which deal with more significant matters:

*Special Office*

There are a number of Special Offices around the country which are staffed by senior and experienced Inspectors of Taxes. They deal with complex cases or those which have some difficult aspect to them and it is the Special Offices that usually initiate specific drives or investigations into certain areas.

## Special Investigations Section

This section deals specifically with tax avoidance, mainly involving tax avoidance schemes of an artificial nature. You will not be concerned with Special Investigations Section unless you are involved in some complex tax avoidance arrangements – in which case you will certainly already be professionally advised.

## Enquiry Branch

This is the largest and the most serious investigative office of the Inland Revenue and consists of highly trained Inspectors of Taxes and professional accountants. It is concerned only with large scale evasion and fraud including criminal investigations. Enquiry Branch will become involved only if the figures are large, or if the suspect is a professional tax adviser; they work on the principle that a crooked tax adviser probably has many clients who are not dealing with their tax affairs properly (after all he is advising them) and the pickings for the Inland Revenue are therefore potentially very large.

Enquiry Branch will also become involved if there is evidence of any crime (e.g. forged or false invoices) or conspiracy (e.g. collusion to defraud the Inland Revenue) or if somebody who has been investigated and then reached a settlement with the Inland Revenue is later found to have been concealing material information. When this happens, as it did in the case of Lester Piggott, a criminal prosecution becomes a real possibility.

In addition there is the Investigations Unit (which deals with certain Special Offices), the Special Trades Investigations Unit (which deals with particular areas of industry) and the PAYE Audit Team (who go round checking that employers operate PAYE correctly). These all perform different parts of the investigative functions of the Inland Revenue.

Between them these offices have the resources to deal with most of the problems that can be thrown at them by taxpayers and their advisers, but in addition there are various specialist divisions dealing with stamp duty, inheritance tax, and before it was abolished, development land tax, as well as the various Head Office specialists within the Inland Revenue Technical Division at Melbourne House in the Aldwych.

If you become involved with any of the branches of the Inland Revenue outside the tax district dealing with your affairs you should be on your guard and at least consider taking immediate professional advice.

This book does not therefore dwell on these specialist offices to any significant extent, but is confined to the more ordinary circumstance of dealing with your normal tax office. However that does not mean that the local tax office is staffed by numb-skulls and that all the brains are in these specialist offices. After a tour of duty in these other offices the specialists often end up in ordinary tax districts so you may well find your local Inspector of Taxes is a real expert. Do not underestimate him.

## Inland Revenue Procedures

An explanation of the way the tax system operates may be a useful starting point. Usually the first thing that happens is that at the end of a tax year the Inspector of Taxes sends you a tax return; you fill it in and send it back. You are supposed to send it back within 30 days but that time limit is never enforced and the Inland Revenue do not even expect it to be complied with. If everybody did send in their tax returns within 30 days they could never cope with the work anyway. Nothing will happen unless your tax return is not submitted by 31 October. At that point the Inland Revenue will begin to regard you as being neglectful and they will charge you interest on any tax which ends up being paid late as a result of your delay. The authority for the taxman charging you interest is exactly the same authority which enables him to charge penalties but at the moment they have given no indication that penalties will be imposed if this 31 October deadline is not complied with. However, it probably will not be long before they do.

If you cannot send in your tax return by 31 October because you do not have all the information necessary to complete it by that date (and it is by no means always easy to collate all the information necessary for your tax return within such a short period), you will be protected if you write to the Inland Revenue explaining the position and giving them details of any capital gains you have made and any new sources of income. If you do this there should be no need for the taxman to delay charging you tax and no interest should arise.

It is not enough to keep quiet if you have not been sent a tax return. Everybody is under a statutory duty to notify the Inland Revenue of a source of income whether they have received a tax return or not, so there is nothing to be gained and a great deal to be lost by not saying anything. You will end up paying interest on the tax you should have paid as well as a penalty; this is explained in more detail in chapter 9.

Nor is it any use putting 'to be advised' or 'to follow' or 'not yet ascertained' on your tax return – or even 'per accounts' unless accounts are actually enclosed. These entries are regularly made on tax returns but all they do is show that you are failing to supply the necessary information. If you simply do not know, make reference to the missing figures in your covering letter, preferably with an explanation for the delay and an estimate of what the figures might be. This should protect you in the event that the taxman turns nasty – or if you have inadvertently made some other omission.

So having sent in your tax return or made the relevant notification of income or capital gains, you can expect the taxman to raise an assessment charging you to tax. If you do not send in your tax return he will eventually get round to sending you an assessment anyway on an estimated basis. It goes without saying that his estimate is unlikely to be lower than your true liability; he is not daft. He may also make lots of enquiries and raise another assessment later charging more tax (and interest and penalties) if he is not satisfied that he has everything he needs to determine your tax liability.

If you do not agree with the assessment you have received you must appeal against it stating your grounds, and apply to postpone some or all of the tax. You will need to explain to the Inspector of Taxes exactly why you think the assessment is wrong. He will write to you about it and after some correspondence you will either come to an agreement with him, or your appeal will need to be heard by an independent appeal tribunal, the General Commissioners (or possibly the Special Commissioners). At the appeal hearing the Commissioners listen to what the Inspector of Taxes says and his justification for the tax charged, and then listens to your explanation why you feel the tax is too high. The most important point to appreciate here is that the assessment will stand unless you can prove that it is excessive. The Inspector of Taxes has to prove nothing – the onus is entirely on you. Many people pay more tax than they need simply because they think that it is up to the Inland Revenue to show that their assessment is right. This is completely wrong and unless you appreciate it before you start you may have to learn the hard way.

At the end of the appeal hearing the Commissioners will give their decision and that will usually be the end of the matter. There is an opportunity to appeal to the High Court but that is beyond the scope of this book. For most purposes the Commissioners' determination will be final.

The above gives a broad outline of the procedure in connection with your tax affairs. Each element of this procedure will be examined in later chapters to show where things can go seriously wrong and what opportunities you have for advantage.

# Chapter Two

# MATTERS OF PRINCIPLE

Avoidance or Evasion
Outwitting the Taxman
The Constitutional Position
The Taxpayers' Charter
Concessions
An Unpalatable Truth

# MATTERS OF PRINCIPLE

## Avoidance or Evasion

One of the most talked about distinctions in connection with tax is the difference between tax avoidance and tax evasion. The distinction is of the utmost importance because there is all the difference in the world. At its simplest, tax avoidance is the reduction of tax liabilities by legitimate arrangements, while tax evasion is not paying tax by dishonest means. This is why the difference between the two concepts has been described as the thickness of a prison wall. However, this simple formulation does not adequately deal with the grey areas and perhaps this is why these terms are not used in any technical sense, but only as colloquialisms. Indeed there is a famous tax case in which even an eminent law Lord appears to have confused them.

It is important to work on the basis that the Inspector of Taxes is going to find out everything, so your plans for tax saving must stand up to scrutiny – otherwise they will fall down. A tax saving scheme which involves concealing information from the Inland Revenue is not a tax saving scheme at all, it is a scheme for defrauding the Inland Revenue, (i.e. tax evasion) and it may land you up in court. Those who are skilful in tax matters can often save tax by persuading the taxman to agree with their suggestions. However those who do not have the knowledge or the technique will not get their way by consent and may resort to other means, i.e. dishonest evasion. The acid test, and one which you should bear in mind in all your tax affairs is – are you acting honestly? If you do not know, or cannot tell, the difference, you should ask yourself whether or not, if you explained everything fully to the Inland Revenue you would lose the argument and pay the tax which you are trying to save.

That is not to say you should always bare your soul to the Inspector of Taxes on every occasion that you do anything connected with your tax affairs, but you should never conceal material information. If you do, and if you are found out, you will be in trouble. Ignorance can be bliss, but not for Inspectors of Taxes. Keeping them in the dark will often mean that you end up paying rather a lot of interest and penalties.

The position with professional advisers is much more sensitive. The Inland Revenue have continual dealings with lots of professional advisers and their experience of any particular adviser will be very important indeed in determining whether you have an easy time, or a great deal of bother, with the taxman. The taxman will be able to judge from his experience of the professional adviser whether he is competent, knowledge-able and honest, and you should always make sure that your professional adviser is all three. If the taxman thinks that your accountant can be relied on you will be given a lot more benefits of doubts than otherwise. When he puts forward information on your behalf to the taxman, it is far more likely to be accepted as being reliable and the taxman will rarely seek proof, because he trusts the accountant to have done his job properly. The Inspector of Taxes knows that the professional adviser has a duty to do the best for his client and he will respect competence. Inspectors of Taxes are human and quite capable of recognizing and admiring a job well done, which can only be to your advan-tage. He might not always accept everything your accountant says of course, but if it comes to a dispute, the debate ought to end up as a professional matter with both sides respecting the other's point of view. From this stance you will rarely end up being seriously disadvantaged.

On the other hand if the Inspector of Taxes has reason to doubt your integrity or that of your adviser he will be certainly on his guard in case he is being tricked, and you can expect a really hard time. You will be called upon to prove everything you put forward with the result that the possibility of any advantageous compromise on a problem will simply not arise. The Inspector of Taxes has a great deal of power and this can be exercised very readily against anybody who he feels is not being straight with him. And this does not only apply to you yourself; if your adviser is well known to the Inland Revenue as being a person who sails close to the wind and whose representations when enquired into are often shown to be rather optimistic, if not downright wrong, this will affect the view he takes of all that adviser's clients. You may be squeaky clean but if your adviser is suspect you will still suffer.

To avoid tax successfully you must work within the rules, arranging matters so that you satisfy the technical requirements for whatever you are seeking to claim. It may be that you are claiming a relief or an exemption, or that some receipt is not taxable at all or perhaps at a lower rate of tax; perhaps the most common example is a claim for a tax deduction for certain expenditure. Most of these matters will involve negotiations with the taxman who will make lots of enquiries into the facts surrounding your claim so you need to prepare yourself well and to develop your arguments and strategy in advance. In Chapter 8 some guidance is given about how the negotiations can be conducted to your best advantage but always remember that the Inspector of Taxes can and will keep on asking questions and seeking more facts until he is satisfied that you are entitled to whatever relief you are claiming.

## Outwitting the Taxman

If you really believe you can outwit the taxman you should think again. It is occasionally possible but not at all likely. You may do something once which by fluke or good fortune (or default on the part of the Inland Revenue) may not be challenged. You cannot rely on it and would be foolish to do so unless you have some assurance that the reasons behind the result were soundly based in law or practice. The batsman who edges a ball from Malcolm Marshall through the slips for 4, does admittedly score a boundary but that is not quite the same as a majestic drive through extra cover. The entry in the score book is the same but one could easily draw a false conclusion.

The taxman is an expert in tax law and practice and, what is more, he has detailed instruction manuals and technical back-up within the Inland Revenue to help him get the answer right. Furthermore he has a great deal of experience of taxpayers who try not to reveal or pay tax on all sorts of income. His whole career is likely to have been spent doing this and he will have come across most of the ruses you will ever think of. To put it another way he knows much better how to fiddle the taxes than you do. If you are planning or hoping to fiddle your taxes just pause for a moment's reflection. It is a very complex subject and you do not know the rules, but your opponent does; indeed he is a trained expert.

How then do you think you can pull the wool over his eyes? Nearly all ideas for doing so are based on the premise that the taxman will never be able to find out about something – you can string him a line and he will not be able to know whether it is true or false. It is explained in Chapter 6 that the taxman is very likely to find out anyway and unless you really know what you are doing and are prepared to deliberately embark on a criminal enterprise you face an uphill struggle.

If the taxman is going to find out about what you are up to and will discover that you have some money you were trying to conceal, you are in trouble. It would be better to concentrate on the ways in which the particular money may quite legally not be liable to much, or any, tax. You might want to argue that, for example:

a)  It is not your money – it really belongs to somebody else; or
b)  It is not taxable at all because of some technicality; or
c)  You have lots of expenses to set against it which reduce or exhaust the income.

Let us look at each of these in turn with the help of an illustration. You work as a computer salesman with a large computer company and earn a reasonable salary which puts you well into the higher rate of tax. In your spare time you have helped your neighbour set up a computer system for his business and he has paid you £10,000 because your work was so good and it saved him a lot of money. You arranged for the money to be paid to a friend – the friend is going to give you the money back later but in the meantime he puts in his bank. This simple set of circumstances gives rise to some interesting implications. It is very likely that the neighbour who paid the money is almost certainly going to want to deduct the £10,000 in his business accounts because he is entitled to tax relief for the payment (it is a valid business expense) and he is not going to forfeit a tax saving of possibly £4,000 just to help you conceal it from the Inland Revenue – quite apart from the fact that by doing so he may lay himself open to charges of conspiracy by trying to help you. The taxman is likely to ask him to whom he paid the money and if he refuses to tell them (or says he cannot remember) he will get a very old fashioned look from the taxman. The first thing which will happen is that he will be denied tax relief. The next possibility is that the Inland Revenue's PAYE Audit team will pay him an early visit and suggest that this amount must have been a payment of wages or salary to an employee which should have had PAYE and NIC deducted. A salary of £24,000 would give rise to PAYE and NIC of approximately £14,000 leaving the £10,000 paid to the unknown individual. So, the Inland Revenue will demand £14,000 being the tax and national insurance contribution which should have been deducted from the earnings and will add interest and penalties for failing to submit a proper PAYE return at the relevant time. This would stretch the neighbour's goodwill a little too far so he will almost certainly provide details of the work done and the payment made. The taxman will then send a note to the Inspector of Taxes dealing with your tax return and if he finds that you have not put the income on your tax return you will be in trouble. So we must return to the three arguments referred to above.

a) The money belongs to somebody else. The argument here is that it was paid into somebody else's bank account and that other person has nothing to do with you. The first problem here is that it is not true – and you know it. You know the money is really yours and the only reason you are suggesting otherwise is in the hope of saving some tax. It is always the first lie which is the most crucial. Once this is put forward you are in a real fix because you can never deny it later without admitting deliberate deception. Once you have admitted attempting deliberately to deceive the Inland Revenue they will never again believe a word you say (and why should they?). The Inspector of Taxes will therefore raise an assessment on you for the £10,000 and the onus will then be on you to show that it is wrong. For good measure they will probably raise an alternative assessment on your friend who received the money and he will not thank you for getting him caught up in all this.

However, let us think a little further about the position here because if tax law is properly applied to the circumstances you will see that the whole argument is a dead end anyway. You could say that you worked for the neighbour in return for him paying nothing to you but £10,000 to somebody else. This is quite possible – maybe you owed somebody else £10,000 and this was a means of arranging for the debt to be paid off. A moment's thought is all that is required to realize that this is a hopeless point. It would be no different from asking your employer to pay your mortgage repayments in return for not having a higher salary. So even if it were true, no tax would be saved and there would be a cruel irony in putting forward a false story exposing yourself as a dishonest person, when even if the falsehood was accepted it would not save any tax.

So we can move on to the next point:

b) It is not taxable at all because of some technicality.

Without professional advice you have very little chance of arguing it successfully. Nevertheless there is some scope here – although the Inland Revenue never like to accept that any receipt is tax-free. A possible argument would be that it was a gift, a personal matter between neighbours unconnected with the actual work done and therefore not in the nature of taxable income at all. The payment may have been made as a gratuitous gesture because you had been so kind to your neighbour and demonstrated your fine personal qualities. This may sound a little fanciful but there could be an element of truth in it and obviously it would need to be expertly argued – perhaps resulting in a negotiated settlement with the Inland Revenue that only part of it should be taxed. There is nothing wrong or disadvantageous in following this line but what is important is that you do not conceal the receipt from the Inland Revenue and that you put all your cards on the table. Concealment will irrevocably damage the credibility of your argument. If the Inland Revenue have to find out about it themselves before you admit to the receipt they will not unnaturally assume that you have no real belief in the argument at all and that therefore it is probably only a fabrication put up for the purpose. This is not a good stance upon which to begin negotiations. The receipt is bound to come out anyway so you might as well disclose it and face up to the argument early – and by putting it forward confidently you would be able to start the argument with the initiative.

c) You may have lots of expenses to set against the income.

Again this line is one where professional advice will be worthwhile. If the amount is taxable there may be various deductions you can set against the receipt to reduce the tax payable on it. First, however, you need to identify why it is taxable and the most likely answer is that you were acting as a freelance computer business consultant. If so, you may have had to buy things to enable you to act in this capacity – magazines, special parts to help with the neighbour's problem, maybe telephone calls to friends to help on particular points, or you may have worked on it at home, thereby enabling you to claim a proportion of your home expenses against the amount received.

These three arguments are just examples of how a problem of this nature can be approached with the taxman. It will be apparent that if you are going to win the point you have to think through the whole of the implications before you start. Trying to get the better of the taxman without a clearly planned strategy will nearly always be a waste of time, and you might even find yourself in a worse position than if you had never tried in the first place.

## Tricks

Those who play with fire do not get their burns treated with any sympathy and the same goes for taxpayers (and particularly their advisers) who play tricks with the Inland Revenue. I do not mean taking advantage of the rules or the procedure, of which this book contains many examples, but sharp practices and things that the taxman likes to call 'obfuscation'. This is a euphemism for misrepresentation accidentally on purpose. One example recently quoted was of a taxpayer who claimed a tax deduction for a 'water storage tank' which on further enquiry turned out to be a swimming pool. Such excesses of imagination will land you in trouble – although probably only interest and penalties. However if you buy a suit and put it in the accounts as curtains you may end up in court.

Another favourite is to include round sum estimates in account but then to 'de-round' them by adding or subtracting 1 or 2 – so that £1000 becomes £998 or £1002. By doing this you can make what is really a round sum estimate look as if it is an accurate and carefully calculated figure. The taxman will tend to enquire into estimated figures but the spuriously accurate figures created by the de-rounding will mislead him into believing the figures are not estimates. This particular ploy is regarded by the taxman as a deliberate attempt to defraud and if he finds out, you can expect a visit from two rather aggressive gentlemen who tell you that you are not obliged to say anything but what you do say will be taken down . . . .

Examples of sharp practices like this are limited only by the ingenuity of man, and some are referred to elsewhere in this book. They all have one consequence in common which is that once you are rumbled (and usually it only takes one question) you will certainly face an in-depth investigation going back at least 6 years. Furthermore you will be a marked man and nothing you say to the taxman in the future will be accepted at face value.

That one question is rather important and ought to be considered very carefully. If you are contemplating some trick (or worse) just give some thought to the question the taxman would have to ask to defeat your purpose. It will not be difficult. Then think of all the reasons why he might ask it and what other questions would lead him unerringly in the right direction. You may find that your plan rests on rather a knife edge. You might get away with it, but there again the chances might not look too good – and the downside is a horror story.

## The Constitutional Position

The battle with the taxman is an example of the relationship between the State and the citizen and the levying of taxes has not surprisingly played an important part in the development of our constitutional law. Magna Carta in 1215 had something to say about it but it was in the 17th century that things really started to happen. In Bates Case 1606, a merchant refused to pay a duty on the import of currants, contending that it was contrary to the Statute of Edward III, and in 1627 the defendants in the Five Knights case were imprisoned for refusing to pay a forced loan. In 1637 in the celebrated Ship Money case, John Hampden refused to pay his taxes on the grounds of 'no taxation without representation'. The eventual solution was the Bill of Rights in 1688 which declared that 'levying money for or to the use of the Crown by pretence or prerogative without the consent of Parliament' was illegal. As time went on every development whereby the Crown or Parliament was given the power to take away a man's property was surrounded by numerous constitutional safeguards. It is no less the case today, despite the extremely sophisticated system of taxation, duties, contributions, licences, fines and all the other ways that the state can take away money from the citizen. Indeed there is the added comfort of the European Convention on Human Rights which provides that no one shall be deprived of his possessions except as authorised by law; although the Convention has no legal force in the UK its terms still have a considerable influence.

It is by no means inappropriate to consider the present tax

rules in the light of this constitutional position. It may occasionally afford opportunities for defeating the taxman's claims in strange and unexpected ways. It is in this context that the case of the Council of Civil Services Unions v. Minister for the Civil Service (1984) is of considerable importance.

In 1983 the Prime Minister gave an instruction under the Civil Service Order 1982 for the variation of the terms of employment of staff at GCHQ at Cheltenham to the effect that they would no longer be permitted to belong to a national trade union. This caused a considerable uproar and after a long legal battle the House of Lords decided that the Prime Minister's decision could not be interfered with because it was based on grounds of national security. What is interesting and relevant about this case in terms of taxation is the reasoning of their Lordships in reaching this decision. (Incidentally the circumstances also gave rise to a tax case because those who accepted the variation in their terms of employment were paid £1,000 and the question arose whether this amount was taxable. It was, but that is not a matter of major significance.)

Deep in the minutiae of their Lordships' judgement they express various views about the conditions to be satisfied before a decision made by the administration can be open to review by the Courts. Where the executive in exercising a statutory power does something affecting the rights of the citizen, that power may be challenged by the Courts. This is the means by which the Courts can control what would otherwise be an unfettered executive discretion by central or local government. The House of Lords said that the decision by the administrative body can be reviewed (and in appropriate cases quashed), if it has consequences for the citizen which, among other things, deprive him of some benefit or advantage which he has in the past been permitted by the administrative body to enjoy and that he could legitimately expect to be permitted to continue until there had been communicated to him some rational grounds for it being withdrawn.

You may wonder what this has to do with the ordinary man sending in his tax return, but consider the following circumstances. You are sent a tax return early in the tax year and on the front it says that it must be completed and returned within 30 days. You do not get round to sending it in until October. You are clearly in default and the taxman has lots of powers under the Taxes Acts to charge you a penalty for failing to send in your tax return on time. This is obviously a simple example and the Inland Revenue would rarely if ever suggest that you should be penalised for such a delay. But what would you do if they did seek to impose a penalty? According to the statute you would have no defence at all. You are required by law to send in your tax return within 30 days and there are penalties for not doing so. How can you say that the Inland Revenue is in the wrong by applying the law? This is where the principles behind the CCSU case come into play. You could reasonably say, and you would succeed, that you have in the past been allowed the benefit of such a delay and you had a legitimate expectation that it would be allowed to continue unless and until you had been notified that it had been withdrawn. On these grounds you could confidently expect to escape any penalty – unless of course the Inland Revenue had written to you earlier saying that they would no longer be allowing such delays in the submission of your tax return. (In this context, it is interesting to note that the Inland Revenue have issued a statement saying that they will, contrary to law but as a matter of practice, allow tax returns to be submitted within 12 months without any penalty, although this is modified in the case of capital gains and new sources of income which have to be notified to the Inland Revenue by 31st October following the tax year in which the capital gain is made or the new source of income arises.)

This principle can be extended to more complex circumstances such as the submission of business accounts and all other more specialized returns, or the adoption of various concessionary practices regarding the taxation of certain income. There are any number of strange customs such as the preparation of accounts on the cash basis, or perhaps a special treatment you may have negotiated with the taxman regarding various allowable expenses in your circumstances, and any withdrawal of these arrangements without notice may well give you reasonable grounds for complaint. You can hardly object to the taxman telling you he is going to apply the law in future but you can successfully resist him penalizing you for previously failing to comply with the law, if by his actions he has knowingly allowed you to do so. The judgement in the CCSU case is unlikely to save you any imposition of any interest and penalties if you have been in default, but if not it will at the very least allow you a good negotiating platform from which to reach a favourable settlement with the Inland Revenue.

## The Taxpayers' Charter

This is a most important document which was issued by the Inland Revenue in 1986, setting out in general terms the manner in which the Inland Revenue staff are expected to deal with taxpayers. It contains some remarkable statements which can be used to great effect if you get into difficulty with the Inland Revenue. It is well worth reading in full (and you will almost certainly have been sent one) but the following extracts are particularly important.

a) You are entitled to expect that the Inland Revenue will help you in every reasonable way to obtain your rights and to understand and meet your obligations under the tax laws.

This is very helpful because if you fail to make some claim or other which is obviously to your advantage, and is clear from information you supplied to the tax man, you can at the very least suggest that he ought reasonably to have told you about it. Tax is notoriously complex and you cannot be expected to know all the available reliefs and exemptions and all the conditions behind them. If you are denied your claim on some technical grounds there could be a good reason for you to say that the Inspector of Taxes has not helped you in the way you are entitled to expect. Similarly, if you fail to do something (i.e. you are neglectful) because you misunderstood the position and they charge you penalties as a result, you should draw attention to the fact that you were entitled to be helped to understand your obligations and that help was not forthcoming. On this ground you can reasonably claim that penalties should not be imposed. There are many occasions where people have been spectacularly successful in being relieved from tax (let alone interest and penalties) by arguing hard and long that their failure was really the fault of the Inland Revenue who should have been more helpful.

In return for this obligation the taxman does require that you will give him the full facts about your affairs. This is wholly reasonable – you cannot expect him to point out that you should make a claim for something if he has not got all the information. Any piece of relevant information which he has not been given will allow him grounds for saying that he did not know whether the claim you are after would be to your advantage or not.

b) Courtesy and compliance: The staff of the Inland Revenue will at all times carry out their duties courteously, considerately and promptly.

This is the sort of general statement that one might expect from a government department and you may well feel it is meaningless. However, that would be to ignore the possibility of advantage in times of trouble. Chapter 11 explains how to handle the rude and aggressive taxman and here is the official condemnation of such behaviour. The Inspector of Taxes who is discourteous is not just an unpleasant person, he is specifically in breach of the Taxpayers' Charter; the same applies if your affairs are not dealt with promptly. It is likely that you will encounter one or other of these failings sooner or later in your dealings with the Inland Revenue. There is unfortunately no sanction or remedy for breaches of the Taxpayers' Charter, and if you meet a rude taxman or suffer inordinate delays with your correspondence, there is very little that you can do. You have not been particularly disadvantaged – just inconvenienced or insulted.

However, it can reasonably be assumed that the Inland Revenue put these words in the Taxpayers' Charter for a purpose and although what it is might be difficult to discern, *in extremis* you can suggest any reasonable purpose. Imagine for example that you have been waiting a long time for a reply to your letter and you end up receiving an unsatisfactory and discourteous response. (By discourteous I do not mean that it is necessarily just rude – I mean that it ignores the points you have made or otherwise dismisses your arguments without reason.) You might justifiably complain that you were so put off by the taxman's approach that you were late in making your claim (or whatever) or that the taxman's lack of promptness was a contributory factor to you missing a time limit; alternatively you can say that you failed to notify the Inland Revenue of something because of his lack of courtesy and his inconsiderate conduct. This may only be partly successful but when you are under pressure from the Inland Revenue, you need every bit of ammunition you can find.

c) You will be presumed to have dealt with your tax affairs honestly unless there is reason to believe otherwise.

This hardly needs to be said, but it is helpful that it is written down so clearly. There may be occasions when the Inspector of Taxes makes enquiries which you can reject on the basis that his enquiries presume dishonesty on your part; it is often not difficult to interpret Inland Revenue enquiries in this way. You will then be able to enquire whether he has reason to believe that you have been other than honest. This will cause him to stop and think because he will not lightly accuse you of dishonesty. Either way he must have grounds and you are able to ask him what those grounds are. He will not want to do so because he might simply be on a fishing expedition but be unable to admit it.

   d) You will be treated in the same way as other taxpayers in similar circumstances.

It is a common complaint that some people get better treatment from the Inland Revenue than others. However, that will not be by design, but just a natural consequence of the need to have different taxpayers dealt with by different Inspectors of Taxes. It is no good saying that your friend next door was allowed to claim tax relief for his new carpets as a business expense because he works at home. This will not get you anywhere but it will probably mean that your friend will lose his tax relief and be investigated into the bargain. What this statement does mean is that if there is a well known practice which applies to certain circumstances, you should not be denied it, and if you are, you can insist that you are given the benefit of the practice or concession. Concessions are dealt with in more detail below.

   e) The Inland Revenue will have regard to the compliance costs of different taxpayers (including the particular circumstances of smaller businesses).

This is a very useful statement to have up your sleeve when you are in lengthly correspondence with the taxman because you can claim quite easily that the burden of compliance on you is onerous and that you simply cannot afford to fight your good case because of costs. This will not mean that the Inland Revenue gives up and allows your claim but you may very well obtain a valuable compromise by pursuing this line – especially if you are a small business. The words in brackets presumably mean that they will be particularly sympathetic to small businesses and you can reasonably work on that basis; however, if you get into difficulties you can ask an Inspector of Taxes what the words are supposed to mean and almost whatever he says in response, you will be able to use it in reaching a favourable settlement.

A number of references are made elsewhere in this book about tactics to be deployed in negotiating with the Inland Revenue particularly in default matters and the Taxpayers' Charter is certainly a valuable weapon in the taxpayer's armoury. It is not well liked by the average Inspector of Taxes and if you can encourage him to fly in the face of it, or even better to make some indiscreet and disparaging statement about it, you will be able to use those indiscretions to end up with a much better conclusion than otherwise.

## Concessions

As tax laws are of such complexity, they give rise to all manner of anomalies. Consequently it is the long-standing practice of the Inland Revenue to alleviate hardship arising from a strict reading of the law by making administrative concessions. The courts have always made disparaging comments about these practices and rightly suggest that there is something decidedly unsatisfactory about the Inland Revenue relieving certain people from tax which is properly payable under the law. The trouble with concessions is that they are not law and cannot therefore be relied on by the taxpayer, and neither can they be enforced through the courts like law – at least not directly.

One particular problem with extra-statutory concessions is that they are only given on the specific condition that they will not be applied in any case where an attempt is made to use them for tax avoidance. It has never been made clear to anybody what possible purpose a concession has other than to enable the person claiming it avoid a liability to tax which would otherwise arise under the strict rules, so their application is somewhat restricted. If, however, you unwittingly get caught up in a tax liability through ignorance of the correct rules, a concession can help you because it will be applied, or can be claimed, providing you meet its specific terms. Although the concessions are not law and therefore cannot be enforced in the courts, what you can do is to insist that you are not denied the benefit of a published Inland Revenue concession on the grounds of natural justice. Quite apart from the fact that it would be a breach of the Taxpayers' Charter, you are entitled to claim that denial of a concession which the Inland Revenue has announced will be available in certain circumstances, is an improper use of the administration's discretionary power and the courts can and will enforce its application on your behalf. However, you do have to go through an enormously complex High Court procedure known as an application for judicial review if you feel that you have been wrongly denied a concession, and the outcome can never be certain.

Therefore, if you are faced with a problem where a relief or other exemption from tax is simply not available under the strict rules, it is well worth obtaining a copy of the Inland Revenue booklet on concessions (known as IR 1) free from any tax office because this booklet sets out the full range of the concessions operated by the Inland Revenue. There are over 130 concessions dealing with all types of situation and whilst some of them are highly technical, others are comparatively simple, such as the flat-rate allowances for some occupations which are given without the need to supply any evidence.

An example which can be extremely valuable is concession A19 dealing with arrears of tax which have arisen because of some official error. This concession has a long history and states that the Inland Revenue will not collect tax if the taxpayer is faced with an unexpected tax demand because of some delay or error by the Inland Revenue. This has much in common with the Taxpayers' Charter but is much more detailed. In essence, if you receive an unexpected tax demand and you have sent all the necessary information to the Inland Revenue in good time, they will let you off all or part of the tax on the grounds of hardship if your income is within certain limits. The income limits are increased regularly but at the time of writing if your gross income is less than £8,500 (£11,000 if you are over 65 or are in receipt of a widow's pension) the whole of the tax will be remitted. If your income is between £8,500 and £23,000 (£25,500 if you are over 65 or in receipt of a widow's pension) a sliding scale applies. In addition, 'special consideration' will be given to those with large family responsibilities. This is a very valuable concession but you must show that all the necessary information

had been provided to the Inland Revenue in good time; if you are
in arrears with your tax affairs you will therefore be in some
difficulty in escaping a tax charge even if it is delayed but you
may still be able to obtain it if you can successfully argue that
there is some good reason (possibly the Inland Revenue's fault
– not complying with the Taxpayers' Charter perhaps) why the
information had not been provided at the correct time.

Concessions can sometimes get you out of a difficulty but
you should not think that they will solve all your problems.
Nevertheless they are well worth looking at if ever you find
yourself in trouble with the Inland Revenue.

## An Unpalatable Truth

This book will reveal a number of truths which are both
unexpected and unpalatable to those without long experience
of dealing with the Inland Revenue; however, the rules are the
rules. They are made in Parliament so if you are dissatisfied
about the law, write to your MP or to the Prime Minister or
go and lobby at Westminster; don't waste your time telling the
Inspector of Taxes that the rules are wrong, foolish, badly
drafted or anything else – unless of course this helps you in supporting a more favourable interpretation. What you need to do
is to work within the rules and make the very best you can of
them – and to make sure that the taxman does not get the better
of you in circumstances when he should not do so.

However, at the end of the day there is one very important
point to appreciate. If you are in serious dispute with the Inland
Revenue you may need to take your dispute to appeal. Let us
say for example that you have moved house and the taxman
has refused to allow you exemption for Capital Gains Tax on
the disposal of your private residence. Perhaps he has refused
your claim on some technical grounds and you feel he is wrong;
furthermore your accountant says that he is technically wrong
too. You are able to take your case to an independent tribunal
called the Commissioners who will hear both sides and decide
who is right. There are no awards of costs before the Commissioners so you can have your appeal heard knowing that
although your accountant or lawyer will charge you (possibly
quite a lot of) professional fees, that will be the end of the
matter. Unfortunately, you may be in for a disappointment.

You may lose the appeal of course – but worse still you may win. Your joy in proving your case and showing the Inland Revenue that you are right and they are wrong would turn to ashes if they appeal to the High Court against the decision of the Commissioners. The problem here is that it costs really big money to take a case to the High Court and although you may have won before the Commissioners you might very well lose the appeal in the High Court and the legal costs will be enormous; you might even find yourself being liable to pay the Inland Revenue's costs as well. This is mighty serious because you could be risking many times as much in costs as you were ever going to be charged in tax. Commonsense will have gone out of the window and unless you feel like a crusade you will almost certainly have to withdraw and pay the tax. You can approach the Inland Revenue to see if they would agree to waive their costs if they win; you can even ask them to pay your costs (which they do only in rare circumstances), but unless they do, you may end up with a substantial bill for professional fees. In any event, the nature of awards of costs means that even if you win you will not recover all the professional costs which you will have paid.

You can just give up of course – nobody can be forced to defend an appeal against their will if they concede the point and accept the consequences, but that just means that the whole exercise is wasted. If you had lost the appeal before the Commissioners you would have given up and paid the tax – but if you win and the taxman appeals to the High Court you may still have to give up the fight and pay the tax. The professional costs of the hearing and all the preparatory work would be down the drain. Remember too that even if you win the appeal in the High Court the Inland Revenue can always appeal further to the Court of Appeal (and to the House of Lords) and even more agonizing judgements will need to be made about the costs.

The moral behind all this is that when you take a case to the Commissioners you may be risking a great deal more than you thought so you need to be quite sure that you know what you are letting yourself in for. It is for this reason that it is so important to be able to reach a negotiated settlement on a favourable basis with the taxman so that the risks and costs of an appeal are avoided. Even if you feel you are right, and he is wrong, it may make much more sense for you to agree to split the difference or allow him to knock a third or a quarter off your claim, just for an easy life. Negotiation by which you can reach a compromise which does not cost too much has a lot to commend it when the alternative is an expensive and possibly abortive appeal hearing.

*Chapter Three*

# SHOULD YOU HAVE AN ACCOUNTANT?

# SHOULD YOU HAVE AN ACCOUNTANT?

Comparatively few people are professionally represented in connection with their tax affairs. This is strange because there seems to be a widespread belief that those people who have accountants acting for them probably pay less tax than those who deal with everything themselves. Logically this would cause everybody to want to have an accountant. However they are perhaps discouraged by the fees that accountants charge, or they maybe feel that their affairs are too small for an accountant to want to be bothered with them.

The problem is that without professional advice you do not know whether you are paying too much tax. Also, unless you go by personal recommendation, you do not know whether any particular accountant is going to be any good. For this reason many people only go to an accountant when they come up against a problem with the taxman – or when their affairs become so complicated that they simply do not know what to do next. This hit and miss approach is unlikely to do you much good and some guidance is needed about how to decide whether to engage a tax adviser at all, and if so, when.

The first thing is of course cost. Accountants charge fees (sometimes high fees) but with any reputable firm these will invariably be based on the time they spend on advising you and dealing with the taxman on your behalf. Fees tend to be charged at an hourly rate and they will vary depending upon the level of skill and seniority of the person dealing with your affairs. It is a mistake to think that you need to see a partner in the firm of accountants. It is helpful to have an initial interview with the partner if possible; this will at least then give you somebody in authority to whom you can write if you want to make a complaint. Many accountants will not charge for an initial interview – they are keen not to discourage new clients – and in most cases they will be able to tell you immediately whether their work will result in a worthwhile tax saving. You can try to get an estimate of fees from them but that is likely to be met with a standard response – it all depends upon how much time will be needed to deal with your particular case. This cannot be determined in advance because it depends on two factors which the accountant does not know – how good you are at keeping the necessary records concerning your tax affairs and what enquiries the Inland Revenue will make. This is reasonable if looked at from the accountant's point of view. If he quotes you a fee to cover all eventualities it will probably be very high and put you off – if he estimates a low fee and has to spend extra time on your affairs for very good reasons, you will end up with a fee much higher than his initial estimate and you will be dissatisfied when you find out.

You might be comforted by the fact that if he deals with a lot of people like you, he probably charges the right sort of fee – if he did not do so he would have few clients left. What you can do is to ask him what the hourly rates are for various grades of staff; this will not help you very much at the beginning but it will later if you find something has gone wrong and you think he is charging too much. Also ask him what the normal fee is for somebody like you if everything goes according to form and nothing out of the ordinary arises. He ought to be able to do this. If he cannot it is probably because he does not have enough clients like you to be able to make a reasonable estimate – in which case you should go to somebody who does, because he may not be sufficiently experienced in dealing with your particular type of problems.

It is important to appreciate that it is not simply a question of trading off fees against tax saving. You really do need to take a longer term view. One of the reasons you may want an accountant is to be relieved of all the anxiety caused by the constant barrage of communications from the Inland Revenue. Just to re-direct everything to your accountant without a second thought, knowing that he will do all the checking and if anything needs to be done he will tell you, is worthy of a reasonable annual fee. It is called peace of mind. What is equally important, an accountant who deals with matters regularly for you will very considerably reduce the chances of the taxman deciding to turn you over – for example if you make an innocent mistake and forget to put something on your tax return. The taxman does not believe in innocent errors – he is naturally sceptical about errors which always seem to be in the taxpayer's favour.

Should something go wrong, the taxman's initial enquiries will be dealt with by somebody in the accountant's office who knows what they are doing, and the likely consequence of the first stage in the correspondence will be much more to your advantage. The costs may therefore seem like a new overhead and a drain on your limited resources but they do need to be put in perspective – providing you choose the right accountant.

## How to Decide

Trying to find the right accountant from the telephone book is not likely to be very productive. How on earth do you know whether the person you choose is actually any good? The answer is that you cannot, and the best way is to ask a friend or acquaintance about his accountant. You could ask the bank manager, as he will know lots of accountants, but he is unlikely to have any first-hand knowledge of the nitty-gritty work done by them; all the bank manager sees is the partners and the work you are concerned with would be done by subordinates. The bank manager will therefore rely on his own judgement and the reputation of the particular firm. What you want to know is how the accountant or the subordinate who will be actually dealing with your affairs performs for people like you. So a friend who has an accountant is the man to ask. What you are looking for is a friend who says that he has real confidence in his accountant. Don't take too much notice of stories about wonderful feats of tax saving which have been achieved – they may or may not have been embroidered. What you want is somebody sound in whom you can have complete trust. After all you are going to tell this accountant all the intimate details about your financial affairs (and probably your personal affairs as well) and you want to be able to confide in him and take his advice. It is no good having an adviser if you are going to have doubts about taking his advice. So having got the name of somebody go and see him and see if he is the sort of person you want to deal with.

## Having got one

Having signed yourself up with an accountant you will still not have any idea at first how he is performing on your affairs. However, if you have chosen carefully you should have a degree of confidence in what he is telling you. You should keep alert to various pointers to see if he is doing all he should. If when you ring up it is difficult to find anybody who actually knows anything about your case you should begin to get anxious. Ask for a resumé of the current situation with your tax affairs – if it does not arrive, insist or turn up in person and enquire; after all you are the client and you are paying the bill and the accountant is supposed to be serving you – not the other way round. If you get demands from the taxman which you do not expect ask what is going on. There may be a good reason why something has not been dealt with and a little delay here and there is inevitable – and not necessarily disadvantageous; furthermore the taxman and the Collector of Taxes may have their wires crossed. Tax administration is full of delays and the Inland Revenue do take an inordinate time to deal with things; there is also very little liaison between the Collector of Taxes (who collects the money) and the Inspector of Taxes who decides how much should be paid.

A good indication of whether your accountant is dealing competently with your affairs is when a tax charge arises unexpectedly for more than you thought. Consider carefully any explanation you are given and be on your guard if your accountant says that nothing can be done about it. This may well mean that the Inland Revenue have the upper hand. You would expect the Inland Revenue to have the upper hand when dealing with you – but not with your professional adviser. What you should hear when a problem arises is an explanation of what the problem is, what the solutions are and which one should be pursued in your particular circumstances. It may be that the professional fees in actually pursuing that particular solution will be disproportionately high and you may not want to go along with it, but the accountant should always be able to say how he could deal with it if you would like him to. If you do not hear this it probably means that he does not know what to do, so you should think about finding another tax adviser who does.

*Chapter Four*

# RESIDENCE AND DOMICILE

# RESIDENCE, ORDINARY RESIDENCE AND DOMICILE

A brief explanation of these concepts is necessary because they are central to the determination of tax liabilities in this country and it is important that they are not confused.

## Residence

Income tax is based mainly on residence and most people will therefore only be concerned with UK tax if they are (or will soon become) resident for tax purposes. There are three main tests for determining whether somebody is resident and you only have to satisfy one of them:

a) A person who is physically present in the UK for more than 183 days in a tax year will always be regarded as resident for that tax year. Days of departure and arrival are generally ignored for this purpose. Where physical presence in the UK is for less than 183 days you cannot be resident under this test but there may be another test which will cause you to be resident.

b) A person who visits the UK for an average of 3 months per annum for 4 consecutive years will be regarded as resident in the UK thereafter. However, if it is clear when he first visits this country that his visits will average 3 months per annum for 4 years he will be regarded as resident from the outset.

c) Where a person has accommodation available for his use in this country he will be treated as resident here for any year in which he sets foot in the UK. Use or ownership of the accommodation is irrelevant; all that matters is that the accommodation is available for his use during his presence here – irrespective of whether it is convenient to visit or otherwise. However, it can be ignored if the person works full time abroad and performs no duties (or only incidental duties) in the UK.

Having looked at the above you may decide that you fall outside the tests but you can still find yourself treated as UK resident. For example you might be outside the UK for the whole of a tax year in which case you do not satisfy any of these tests. Unfortunately there is an additional condition, which is that if you are physically absent from the UK for a whole tax year for the purpose only of 'occasional residence' abroad, that is for a temporary, or perhaps for an itinerant, purpose in other countries, you will still be regarded as resident here. So if you want to become non-resident by being away for a complete tax year, you must make quite sure that you go somewhere specific, for a particular purpose and stay there. Remember too that you can be treated as resident in two (or more) different countries at the same time.

### Ordinary Residence

Ordinary residence has comparatively little relevance for income tax but is the main determinant for capital gains tax, so you do not avoid capital gains tax simply by becoming non-resident – you have to become not ordinarily resident as well.

Ordinary residence is a more difficult concept and is broadly equivalent to habitual residence. Ordinary residence does not require physical presence in the UK and it is therefore possible for a person to be resident in the UK (perhaps by virtue of the existence of available accommodation) but ordinarily resident somewhere else if he normally lives abroad. Similarly it is quite possible for a person to be not resident in the UK by establishing residence in another country, but without losing his UK ordinary residence. However, it is not possible to be ordinarily resident in more than one country at the same time. As a general rule the Inland Revenue will not regard an individual as losing his ordinary residence until he had been abroad for 3 years.

Accordingly, if you are planning to save some capital gains tax by becoming not ordinarily resident, you take a supreme risk if you make your gain before the Inland Revenue have agreed at least provisionally (which they will do shortly after your departure) that you are no longer ordinarily resident in the UK. But do not come back during the 3-year period. When you eventually do come back the Inland Revenue will review the position and decide whether they were right in treating you as not resident on the earlier date; if they decide against you and you have made a big capital gain during your absence you will have a few sleepless nights, because they will be rather keen to charge tax on the gain on the basis that you had not lost your ordinary residence at the time you made the gain.

## Domicile

The concept of domicile is difficult but it has a good deal of importance in connection with taxation because of the enormous tax privileges given to individuals who are not domiciled in the UK. Briefly, a non-UK-domiciled person is only chargeable to UK tax on his foreign income and chargeable gains if the income or the gains are actually brought to the UK – this is called taxation on the remittance basis. If you have enough money in the UK to meet your living expenses you can, as a non-UK-domiciled person, keep all your savings abroad and pay no income tax or capital gains tax unless you bring the money here. Indeed it is not too difficult to arrange for the money to be brought here anyway without any tax but this requires specialist professional advice. Other provisions conferring equally valuable reliefs for Inheritance Tax also apply to non-domiciled persons.

There is a great deal of misunderstanding about the concept of domicile, and in particular how you can get hold of a much more favourable domicile than the one you presently possess. The extent of the misunderstandings and the possible tax advantages are both so great that some detailed explanation of the rules is called for.

It is therefore no surprise that because a non-UK-domiciled individual can live in the UK for a substantial period and pay no tax at all, the whole subject is particularly exercising the mind of the Inland Revenue at the present time; the taxman regards these advantages as excessive and disproportionate. It is one thing to encourage inward investment to the UK by foreigners because it is good for the economy; it is quite another to allow people to come here and live tax-free simply by virtue of their foreign domicile which in many cases is little more than an accident of birth. However, although proposals were issued recently to reduce those overwhelming advantages, nothing came of them and the present situation is likely to continue for some time.

Under these circumstances it is only natural that many people try extremely hard to establish a foreign domicile – who wouldn't if it would mean complete exemption from paying all UK direct taxes? Unfortunately, however, a lack of knowledge about the detailed rules leaves some people to take rather an optimistic view of the whole matter. It takes an awful lot more than just buying a house abroad and living there for part of the year to establish a foreign domicile. What you have to show, and by the nature of things tax you will have to prove, is that you have either a domicile of origin abroad or have acquired a domicile of choice abroad and if you are going to do so you will need to know the rules.

Domicile is not a term specifically defined for tax purposes but takes its meaning from the general law. In general terms it is fair to say that a person is domiciled in the country in which he regards his natural home and where he intends to stay, or return to, permanently. This is a concept not a legal definition so don't think that by monkeying around with the words you will achieve anything.

A domicile of origin is essentially the domicile you are born with; usually it is determined by the domicile of your father at the time of your birth – where you were actually born has little or nothing to do with it. Accordingly if you are claiming to have a foreign domicile of origin you must investigate the circumstances of your parents at the time of your birth – and also take into account what you have done and where you have lived since that date, particularly since you were sixteen which is the age when you are able to acquire an independent domicile. Negotiations with the taxman over domiciles of origin tend to be a purely legal argument and there is not much you can do except to argue skilfully – you cannot alter the facts. If you are claiming to have acquired a domicile of choice you have a good deal more scope because you can conduct yourself in a manner which will improve your argument. However, again it is necessary to know how a domicile of choice is acquired and lost if you are going to have any chance of improving your circumstances. The rule for the acquisition of a domicile of choice is simply stated thus:

'A person acquires a domicile of choice in a country by the combination of residence and the intention of permanent and indefinite residence but not otherwise.'

It is immediately apparent that you cannot possibly have a

domicile of choice in a country unless you actually reside there
– so it is no good claiming a foreign domicile of choice unless you
have at least established a permanent residence in that country.
Secondly you have to show that you have an intention of permanent or indefinite residence in that other country. Intention is
a subjective matter and is therefore difficult to prove. It is not
enough just to say that you have the necessary intent – the
Inland Revenue will require positive proof and an investigation
into your personal circumstances will be necessary.

One point which is fatal to the claim for a domicile of choice
in a foreign country is to have an intention of returning to the
UK in the long term. If you do have such an intention you are
sunk – and if you do ultimately return to the UK the Inland
Revenue are most unlikely to accept that you ever acquired a
domicile of choice while you were abroad. Any indication that
you are retaining long term connections with the UK will
seriously damage your argument and so will frequent visits
here. There is a popular fallacy that buying a burial plot in
another country is all you need to establish a domicile of choice
in that country. There is some underlying sense to the idea but
it is invariably overstated. If you are intending to be buried
in a particular country it does give some indication that you have
in mind a settled intention of staying there until you die but
this is by no means enough – it is just one of the many factors
to be taken into account.

So if you want to stand any chance of saving UK tax
by establishing a foreign domicile of choice you are going to
have to live in that other country, preferably in long-term (not
rented) accommodation and to sever all continuing connections
with the UK – and even then you will have to wait a very long
time. If you think you will be able to snatch the crock of gold by
a mere cosmetic rearrangement of your affairs, think again.

This can be illustrated simply by the case of the late Charles
Clore who moved to Monaco shortly before his death and claimed
to establish a domicile of choice there. He was never happy in
Monaco and often expressed a wish to return to England. He
had taken most of the action which would normally have shown
that he intended to acquire a domicile of choice in Monaco (he had
very high quality advice) but he could never manage to establish
the most important factor – that is, an intention of permanent
residence there.

When you are asked about your long-term intentions by the

Inland Revenue you will need to state firmly and unequivocally that you have no intention of returning to the UK and that you intend to reside permanently in your new chosen territory. However you cannot say this if it is not true. A statement of your intentions which is false is a fraudulent misrepresentation; it may be difficult to prove that your statement was false (rather than that you had merely changed your mind later) but that does not make it, nor its consequences, any less serious if it can be shown to be false.

It is relevant here to point out that a person loses a domicile of choice by the combination of ceasing to reside permanently in the chosen territory and ceasing to intend to reside there permanently, so you should take extreme care in your dealings with the Inland Revenue not to inadvertently give the impression that you have ceased to intend to reside permanently in that other territory, particularly if you are temporarily away from it. Sometime after your arrival in the UK you will be provided with a form P86 by the Inland Revenue which contains a number of questions – and one question is of the utmost importance. It says, 'Do you intend to stay in this country permanently?' This is not a trap, it is an ordinary question but it is still of the utmost importance. If you answer yes, you can forget all about a foreign domicile straightaway; if you answer no you had better be ready to say what your intentions are. In most cases the correct answer is 'I don't know' but this is not the sort of answer which people usually expect to put on a form. Forms tend to be designed for a yes or no answer. But it may be the most accurate answer in your circumstances – it all depends. What you should never do is treat Inland Revenue forms, especially form P86, with disdain because your answer here could have the most far-reaching consequences on your long-term tax position.

If you are in the fortunate position of having a foreign domicile and come to the UK you will face another set of circumstances. You will still need to answer the above question on form P86 and you will need to give it the most careful thought. However, there is a crucial distinction here between a person with a domicile of origin and a person with a domicile of choice. A domicile of origin is amazingly adhesive and will stay with you through thick and thin until you take positive steps to acquire a domicile of choice. You can leave your country of origin vowing never to return, but you will keep your domicile of origin unless and until you acquire a domicile of choice elsewhere. You will immediately see the contrast with a domicile of choice and the ease with which it can be abandoned. Furthermore it should be recognized that if you have a domicile of choice which is abandoned the most likely consequence is not that you acquire a new domicile of choice (which inevitably takes some time) but that your domicile of origin will revive.

What this means is that you can say what you like about your country of origin but providing you do not have an intention to reside permanently in the UK you will keep the non-domiciled privileges, so you should take great care not to conduct yourself in a manner which indicates that you have in fact (whether you say so or not) acquired a domicile of choice here.

*Chapter Five*

# DIFFERENT TAXMEN

# TYPES OF TAXMAN

Reference has previously been made to the fact that there are all sorts of taxmen and it is pot luck which one you get to deal with your affairs. In fact there are as many different taxmen as there are ordinary people but a few of the more commonly encountered examples of the species can be spotlighted. Each of the following examples is drawn from a genuine experience with a real live Inspector of Taxes.

## The Gestapo Type

This type of Inspector of Taxes can be recognised very easily by his extremely aggressive approach. This type knows that he has immense power and enjoys baring his fangs against the hapless taxpayer. He starts from the outset on the basis that the taxpayer is on the fiddle and makes all sorts of assertions which are based on prejudice or unfounded guesswork and probably both. For no reason at all he demands an interview with the taxpayer and makes all sorts of thinly veiled (and sometimes unveiled) threats about the consequences of not acceding to his demands. Such types will never be satisfied until they have wrung out of the taxpayer an addition to his tax bill. This is an extremely difficult example of the species to deal with, mainly because he really does have immense power and must therefore be handled with extreme care.

This type of Inspector will invariably have as little regard for the niceties of the tax rules as he will have for the sensitivities of the taxpayer and this is his Achilles heel. You must lead him into indiscretion bearing in mind always that you are going to have the case reviewed by his superior in due course. But do not be too hasty. You must give him enough rope to hang himself first. Remember that it will be the file which will be reviewed so you must make sure that the file contains lots of things which will show him in the worst possible light and will show you in the best possible light. Overt courtesy in all your correspondence will be seen in stark contrast to his aggressive letters. Make quite sure that you demonstrate every willingness to co-operate with the Inland Revenue at every stage because he will assuredly allege sooner or later that you have been unco-operative simply because you do not do exactly as he says; this is important because lack of co-operation is grounds for increasing penalties if he can find any default. Stay calm and deal with his enquiries but never fail to point out where you feel he is mistaken or is being unreasonable. Make quite sure that you highlight the points where he has failed to deal with your arguments and make your explanation as full as possible. The more indiscretions you can provoke by asking for reasons and justifications for his stance the better case you will have at the end of the day.

The occasional telephone call to the Inspector is usually a good way to elicit indiscretions but make sure that you make full notes of the telephone conversation, verbatim if possible. After a decent interval (i.e. after he has written up his own notes of the telephone conversation) write to him dealing with all the points raised and make sure that you refer to every unfortunate statement he has made. The occasional quotation will be very valuable here. In your telephone conversation it would be very useful to make reference to the Taxpayers' Charter (see Chapter 2) because this is a thorn in the side of such an Inspector and he may well make disparaging remarks about it. Get them all down. (The Taxpayers' Charter was issued by Head Office as a policy statement and it will be greatly to his detriment if on a review of the case he can be seen to have rubbished it.) This will ensure that all the relevant points he has made are on record and (although you will never actually see his notes) your record of what went on might differ considerably from the record that he has made. Your version will not automatically be accepted, in fact it will probably be viewed with suspicion, but if it is wholly consistent with your earlier correspondence it will have the advantage of obvious authenticity which will give it considerable weight. Remember too that his superiors will not be unaware of his aggressive tendencies and this will add substance to your complaints in due course.

The correspondence, notes and discussions may well go on for some time but that does not matter. You need time to develop your arguments, and you might even persuade him to your point of view, but in the end you must be sure that everything in your favour has been said, so that he has no opportunity to say that he has not been provided with enough information, or that you have been unco-operative. When you think you have got as much ammunition as you need you should write to the District Inspector explaining your grievances and say that you intend to refer the matter to the Regional Controller but before doing so you felt it would be courteous to draw the matter to his attention in case he has any comments. This should provoke an immediate reaction. Providing you have filled up the file with all the necessary points to support your expressions of grievance there is a reasonable chance that a discernible change in emphasis will take place and an acceptable solution will be put forward.

It is, however, important to appreciate that this type of approach will be absolutely hopeless if you are in default in any way. If there is something wrong with your tax returns, for example there is some income omitted, you are not in a position to argue if the Inspector of Taxes takes a vigorous approach in trying to ensure that there are no further omissions. In those circumstances all you can do is to suggest that he has gone over the top, but that is much less likely to be successful. If, however, there is nothing obviously wrong with the tax returns or the accounts, this approach will probably pay dividends.

## The Delightful Gentleman

This is a breed which many people feel does not exist in the ranks of the inspectorate but they are entirely wrong. There are a large number of Inspectors of Taxes who are unhesitatingly helpful, courteous and understanding. Some are at a fairly low level of seniority and some are higher but you must make the most of them wherever you find them because they will bend over backwards to reach a reasonable conclusion. They react really well to old-fashioned courtesy and even better to a gentle but firm approach. They do not want to be nasty to anybody and the compromises that can be obtained with such gentlemen can be quite startling. You must not push your luck with these types because the last thing you want is for the file to be reviewed by a less delightful Inspector who decides that his subordinate's approach is far too generous. It does no harm to assume that all Inspectors of Taxes are like this until there is evidence to the contrary and to conduct your correspondence accordingly. If your assumption is right you will start off on the right track and will immediately make a friend who will do his level best to be fair and reasonable to your point of view. If your assumption is wrong and the Inspector turns out not to be at all polite and understanding you will probably get the best out of him anyway by starting out with a courteous approach – you can always harden up later if necessary.

Some years ago I had an experience that I will never forget and which taught me always to be as nice as pie to Inspectors of Taxes – not necessarily to be compliant but courteously to express the opposing view firmly and professionally. I had made a claim for a relief on behalf of a client and the Inspector wrote back to say that he thought the claim was technically unsound and the tax would have to be paid. Correspondence ensued of some complexity and at extreme length but he continued steadfastly to say that his view was right and my view was wrong. In the end, I wrote a really long letter setting out all the arguments in full, acknowledging his good points, asking for his acceptance of my good points and generally suggesting that on balance my claim should be preferred. The best I could really have hoped for is that the Inspector would say that maybe I had a point and that he would therefore allow the claim. Not a bit of it. He wrote back saying that he understood all my points but that his view was much sounder and that the relief was not technically due. However, because of the professional manner in which the problem had been approached and the unfailing courtesy with which the correspondence had been conducted, he would allow the claim. This story, though almost incredible, is entirely true. It taught me always to be as friendly as possible to the Inspector of Taxes because you never know what might happen. Such an occurrence is unlikely to be repeated, particularly in such obvious terms, but it does show that the gentle approach can pay dividends. Not with the Gestapo type of course; you will not wring any concessions out of him – but your courteous and professional approach will show him up as the bad guy when somebody reviews the file.

## The Obstinate Fellow

Some Inspectors of Taxes are perfectly nice chaps but are extremely obstinate and will simply never agree with anything you say. You can argue till you are blue in the face but you are met with a constant demand for more and more information of decreasing relevance. This can drive you wild because there is obviously no end to the questions that an Inspector of Taxes can

ask. It does no good to say that with all the information you have
provided he ought to be satisfied. He will quite rightly say that he
has a statutory duty to be satisfied with your accounts or other
information, and whether you think he ought to be satisfied or
not really has nothing to do with it. You cannot avoid providing
relevant information of course but there will come a time when
you have had enough and you should say so. Summarize the
information you have provided and how it supports your claim,
point out the irrelevant questions he has asked (and that you
have answered) and suggest that if he remains in doubt he really
ought to say what issue needs to be resolved before he will accept
your claim. This will nearly always put him on the spot because
he probably will not know: he just feels generally uneasy. You
must eke out of him what is troubling him and what facts will
enable him to agree. You can then invite him to concede that if
those facts can be proven, he will agree. He is likely to say that
each case depends on its own facts (this is a favourite expression)
in which case you have the clear opportunity to ask him what
the relevant facts are. What you need to get from him is a clear
list of points that he is not happy with. If he is unwilling to do
this, you must do it for him by setting out all the main points
and asking whether he is satisfied with each of them, and if not
what is the nature of, and grounds for, his dissatisfaction. This
will close down the argument into discrete areas which you can
pick off one by one. He can now either withdraw his objections
or agree to a compromise. If that fails you should ask for the
case to be taken to appeal.

An obstinate Inspector is like a donkey and will respond
only to being led – not pushed. The carrot will not necessarily
be a compromise, because you may feel that no compromise is
appropriate in your circumstances, but the prospect of concluding the matter might be extremely attractive to him. Such
Inspectors tend to be under pressure from their superiors for
the number of cases they have open, and if you can offer
him a way of honourably concluding the case, you are in the
driving seat.

## The Ferociously Bright Type

This type of Inspector is one of the most difficult to deal with
but fortunately they are not found in tax offices very often – they

tend to be promoted to higher and better things rather quickly. All you can do with one of these is hope that he will be promoted soon and that a less able colleague will take over. If you spin the correspondence out long enough this will invariably occur but it might take much too long. The ferociously bright Inspector will rarely be of the nasty type. They will have too much confidence in their own abilities to bother being unpleasant. However, he is likely to be really good at thinking up arguments to demolish your case.

You will not be able to discover whether the Inspector is of the ferociously bright variety by mere correspondence; you need to speak to him to discuss the case. Only then will you be able to make a judgement. Before the telephone conversation you should make notes so that you can make some sensible challenges about the points in his favour but at all costs avoid letting him know that you have done a lot of research. Try to have what appears to be an impromptu conversation: if you can make some compelling responses to his points he may think that you are ferociously bright yourself and that will unnerve him. If he is sufficiently well informed to be able to make sensible and equally compelling responses, you will know that he is of a high calibre. The knowledge he shows will be real because he is most unlikely to have done a lot of research immediately prior to your telephone call which will have come out of the blue. If this is the response you receive, you are in real trouble and you must either wait until he is promoted or consider taking professional advice with a view to salvaging something.

## Not Ferociously Bright

Some Inspectors of Taxes are not ferociously bright, indeed not perhaps very bright at all but do not be too optimistic; the dim ones are also pretty rare. The main difficulty with the simple Inspector of Taxes is that he will not understand what you are saying and therefore will not agree with your arguments. (This should be very carefully distinguished from the Inspector of Taxes who understands perfectly what your argument is but rejects it − he is not dim, he just does not agree with your view.) If you do get one of the former it is very tedious because you have to explain everything at extreme length and you get responses which bear no relationship at all to the points you have put forward. It is a bit like speaking or writing to a robot. Sometimes it is as if they have a list of twenty-one answers or statements and they trot these out in order irrespective of their relevance or merit. I remember visiting an Inspector of Taxes once when my case was not particularly good, so I thought I had better have a lot of information about the business at my fingertips. True enough, the questions came thick and fast (well, thick anyway) and full replies were given, but I soon realized that he was not interested in my replies at all – he asked the next question without any comprehension of the answer to the previous one. What was important was that he asked the questions and providing I did not freeze but continued to give a confident response, everything was going to be all right. He never did get round to dealing with the important points.

An Inspector like this is not necessarily an advantage or disadvantage. It could be advantageous because if you are putting forward an optimistic argument, he might not understand the finer points sufficiently to see the flaws in your argument. More likely, and more usually, he will not have enough gumption to use his initiative and may simply write your arguments down and make his replies in correspondence after he has discussed them with a colleague. Alternatively he will go strictly by the book. That would be all right if you knew what his book says but the Inland Revenue do not release their instruction manuals so you do not know and must assume that the strict technical position will be put forward. This is not a problem if you have a plausible technical argument – you may well win providing you lead him gently and irrevocably to your conclusion. However, if you want a concession you will not get it from him because he would be reluctant to stray into such an area. You will have to ask him to see if his District Inspector will be good enough to allow concessionary treatment having regard to your particular circumstances and compelling arguments.

What you must not do is to lose your patience with such an Inspector because that would put him against you and your arguments and turn him into the obstinate variety. Your best bet is to keep explaining in more and more elementary terms how your argument is developed and why it is obviously right; if you can impress him with your analysis he will probably be unnerved. He will know that he is not very bright and if he gets the impression that you are a lot brighter than he is and a lot more knowledgeable, he will be more disposed to accept the view you are putting forward. The well-known British characteristic of shouting loudly at foreigners if they do not understand what you say does not work any better with Inspectors of Taxes who do not understand. Dim or bright, they need to be persuaded that your view is right and not be shouted at.

The big disadvantage with the less able Inspectors of Taxes is that they are nearly always highly diligent and always make the time to do their duty with painstaking tediousness. You can win lots of battles against such specimens but you need to win the war, and this may prove more difficult than it looks. They are rather like slow ferrets and they will usually get there in the end not least because somebody else will probably keep poking them in the right direction.

## Variable Inspectors

I have often experienced an Inspector of Taxes with a fierce reputation as a hard and uncompromising person. With some you can understand why, but with others it is apparent that they have simply been on the wrong end of abuse or unwarranted aggression from the taxpayer or his adviser and they react badly to such treatment, usually by taking a wholly inflexible approach. These Inspectors of Taxes are not really being variable, they are just being human. If you always take an aggressive approach and show him no respect you can kiss goodbye to any concession you may want in the future. There is an old theatrical adage that you should always be nice to everybody on the way up because you will need them on the way down. The same applies with tax matters. You may think that you have a really good opportunity to get the better of, or to humiliate, the Inspector of Taxes but you should resist the temptation. Think of what will happen when you next miss a time limit, or want him to take a flexible approach on a different matter next year. If you don't think you will ever miss a time limit or fail to appeal against an assessment in time, or make a claim for which you almost (but not quite) qualify, then you may not worry, but it is wise to store up a bit of good will which you can call on later.

## The Drunk

Very occasionally you will find an Inspector of Taxes whose intimate relationship with Bacchus leaves him a little worse for wear in the afternoons – particularly on Fridays. In my experience if you can find an Inspector of Taxes in this state you hit the jackpot because they will hang themselves very quickly indeed. You will only be able to discover this through a carefully timed telephone conversation but once you have found him out any problems he may have raised for you are largely over. If you can tell that he is the worse for drink over the telephone, just think about his colleagues; they will be working with him in the same office and will know all about it. The idea here is to provoke indiscretions and to let him know that you know – e.g. by suggesting that you speak to the District Inspector about the technical points he has raised immediately your conversation is finished. Do not complain overtly; he will know much better than you that he does not want to be drawn into conversation with the District Inspector that afternoon. The possibility of him having to see his boss fairly shortly may well have a most helpful effect on his approach and might result (and in my experience has resulted) in an immediate agreement of all outstanding matters. As I say, this does not happen very often but if it does you are on to a winner.

In explaining all these different types I have made great play about the need for courtesy and professionalism in all your approaches to the Inspector. It is not always easy when you think he is behaving like an idiot and refusing to understand the point. But you must try. The Inspector will not (at least not very often) be forced into agreeing with your point of view – he will simply turn into a brick wall. What you really have to do is to persuade him, and that means winning him over to the sense and reasonableness of your argument. Don't just say that he must understand – he won't. You may have to spell it out to him a number of times and probably give it to him in words of one syllable and in a number of different ways. If you adopt the stance that you simply cannot be bothered to explain a lot of obvious points to the Inspector of Taxes then you should not have bothered to start the argument in the first place – you will not succeed. If the point is that obvious and it has not been grasped, you are probably not explaining it very well (in which case you must explain it better). When he does grasp it after your further explanations, he may well feel somewhat embarrassed that he did not see the obvious point before and although he would never admit it to you, it may well encourage him to settle the matter quickly to avoid any further embarrassment.

All this courtesy should not stand in the way of putting forward your views extremely firmly. One way of doing this is to move the argument on to a higher plane. If you treat him as a professional person trying to do his level best to do a proper job and treat the argument as one of principle or academic debate, you can say the most awful things about his views providing it is done nicely. Styles vary of course but in my view using the simple introductory phrase 'With respect' is unlikely to help. This usually means, and is invariably interpreted, as quite the reverse (i.e. no respect at all) and is unlikely to be well received. There is nothing wrong in explaining the opposing arguments and suggesting that his argument is 'poor' or 'unsound' providing you give reasons, and that your view is 'to be preferred' or perhaps that you 'feel confident that any body of Commissioners would understand and accept the argument'. If he completely disregards your arguments, you should insist that he does not do so by suggesting that you feel 'entitled to a response' to the compelling points you have put forward. Imply, but never say, that he has not replied to them because they are too difficult to challenge. Whatever type of Inspector you are dealing with, he is almost bound to have to say something and if he does not, you have excellent ammunition for complaining that he has not dealt with the technical issue fairly.

When asking for the file to be reviewed you have to be extremely careful not to make it sound like an insult and that you are going over his head. In any event you may well find that his superiors will support him simply out of loyalty so you need to exercise great care. You could for example suggest that you have reached an impasse and there are opposing but sincerely held views, the only sensible remedy is for the matter to go to the Commissioners; but before the appeal is listed for hearing it would perhaps be helpful if he had the case reviewed just in case there is an area of compromise or additional arguments (or anything) to enable the precise technical points in dispute to be identified – and of course to clear out of the arena matters in which there is not dispute. This will obviously be necessary before the appeal can properly be dealt with by the

Commissioners. It may do no good but it cannot do your chances of a compromise any harm by showing such confidence in your arguments.

There are of course many other types of taxmen with just as many funny characteristics as ordinary taxpayers. Some are a combination of the above descriptions, and others can change from one to another without warning. It is important to identify the type of taxman you are dealing with because only then can you plan an effective strategy against him.

*Chapter Six*

# DOING A DEAL

# DOING A DEAL

The result of long negotiations with the Inland Revenue is rarely a complete climb-down by the Inspector of Taxes. Sometimes it happens but not often because in the course of a long negotiation he will have usually taken advice and if he was going off the rails he will have been put right. Be on the lookout for indications that advice from his Head Office may have been taken. There may be long gaps between replies and some tell-tale words such as a cryptic opening sentence that the matter has had to be carefully considered. Another revealing sentence is the excuse that 'the file has only recently been returned' – you can guess where it has been.

Another indication that somebody else has become involved is where the Inspector of Taxes suddenly writes a very long letter of a calibre and style which is not entirely consistent with his earlier correspondence. It may well look as if it has been written by somebody else. It will have been. It is important to know this because it may mean that you are no longer dealing with a simple issue with the local Inspector of Taxes, you are fighting Head Office on a matter of principle. The Inspector of Taxes, after being advised by Head Office, may now have no discretion to agree the point at issue; he may be under specific instruction not to agree but to hold fast and if necessary take the matter to appeal, so you would be wasting your time continuing in your efforts to persuade him because he is no longer able to agree. You can waste a lot of time and money and become extremely frustrated at not being able to get anywhere with the Inspector. It sometimes helps to ring him up and find out. You could ask him whether he is under instruction from Somerset House – you have to be ever so discreet and diplomatic but they will often tell you. Indeed on many occasions when speaking to an Inspector of Taxes following complex correspondence I have been told that he understood neither the arguments I was putting forward, nor the replies he was writing in response. In such cases it is much better to try to correspond directly with Head Office and to leave the Inspector of Taxes to get on with all his other work rather than carry on acting as postman.

Sometimes you will receive a letter from the Inspector of Taxes which admits that he has taken advice from his Head

Office specialist who has supported his view, and implies that you should stop arguing. This is a good card for the taxman to play but it is by no means conclusive. This faceless Head Office specialist may or may not be an expert in the relevant subject (he may be new to the department) but in any event that does not mean that he is right. He may be right, but on the other hand he may just be expressing one view supporting the Inland Revenue line and there may be just as good arguments to the contrary. Ask to see the specialist's views – you will not get a copy of his advice but just asking will give you the initiative because a refusal implies that the case may not be as strong as has been suggested. If you are lucky you will sometimes get a summary and possibly details of the relevant authorities provided by Head Office and this can be extremely useful in planning your next approach.

The result of a lengthy negotiation will either be a compromise or deadlock. At all costs you must avoid deadlock because it will lead to confrontation. You can do without a confrontation unless the sums are large. It means that your views are totally rejected and your only remedy is to take the matter to appeal but that is both expensive and risky; it can also have a most unpleasant sting in the tail (see Chapter 2). A compromise is usually the preferred alternative. But you do not get a compromise without careful and skilful negotiation and you may have to completely restructure the arguments in the process. A number of things have to be borne in mind.

The first is that the Inspector of Taxes only really wants to take a case to the Commissioners if he is going to win – or if he thinks he will. What you need to do is to unnerve him sufficiently so that he wants to compromise as much as you do. Simply reiterating your arguments with which you know he does not agree will get you nowhere. What you must do is to cast doubt in his mind. You won't get him to agree with your view but you can make him think that even if he feels he is right, he might not win on appeal. Indeed, you might even cast sufficient doubt in his mind that he wonders whether in fact he is right at all. Taking a case to appeal and losing will do him no good at all. Merely expressing confidence in your whole case will not help – you need to carefully summarize his arguments into the various constituent parts and pick them off one by one. You must not ignore the stronger parts of his argument because those will be the bits he is relying on. You have got to acknowledge his points but indicate that they are outweighed by all the other considerations. You need to think of every reason you can, both technical and non-technical (and analogies if you can find them) why the Commissioners should find in your favour – if only on commonsense grounds. Evidence will need to be given before the Commissioners so consider whether or not all parts of his evidence (or yours) are properly admissible, and whether on a commonsense view they should accept or reject it. For example is it based on gross profit percentages? Do enough of this and the Inspector of Taxes will begin to wonder whether a trip to the Commissioners will be worthwhile.

To take an appeal to the Commissioners involves the Inspector of Taxes in a good deal of preparatory work and puts him under considerable pressure; he has a lot else to do and if he can find a suitable and honourable compromise that would be his best solution. Offer him one – without prejudice of course so that if he rejects it you are not disadvantaged – but always hedge it with indications that you are only being pragmatic and trying to bring the long outstanding matter to a conclusion with justice to both sides etc. Early in my career I used to think that where the issues were clear-cut and there was obviously no middle ground, the possibility of compromise simply did not exist. However, I have come across so many Inspectors of Taxes who are prepared to take a wholly pragmatic view leaving all the technical issues to one side, that I came to the conclusion that nothing is beyond a compromise if you can generate a willingness on his side to accept one.

Throughout the negotiations you must never give any indication that you are not prepared to take the case before the Commissioners. This is a strong card and if it is discarded early by an admission that the case will never go to appeal you lose a major bargaining counter. The Inspector of Taxes will always keep this option open himself and you will negate the effect of this weapon in his hands if you retain the same weapon in yours.

The expression 'doing a deal' perhaps creates a wrong impression because many people seem to think that they can do some kind of trade with the taxman – e.g. if I admit X he will not look into Y. Very few Inspectors of Taxes will countenance any kind of trade-off. You cannot ask him to flout the rules –

you can only ask him to accept your argument in whole or in part as a means of reaching an honourable settlement.(This is not always the case in investigation settlements where there has been some admitted wrongdoing; in those cases there is more scope for flexibility in reaching the ultimate settlement but that is an entirely different matter.)

It must always be remembered that the taxman has a public duty to discharge and you should never put him in a position where he is in danger of failing to do his public duty. That would be just plain daft. If your neighbour managed to persuade the Inspector of Taxes to disregard the rules to his advantage you would feel extremely sore about it; you would say with justification that it is simply not fair – the rules should be operated consistently and fairly between taxpayers. If you do not keep this in mind when you are trying to do a deal you will assuredly fail.

*Chapter Seven*

# SOURCES OF INFORMATION

# SOURCES OF INFORMATION

*Keeping Their Eyes Open*

The Inland Revenue gather their information far and wide. They have amazing sources of information. They have your tax return of course, and the details supplied by your employer, or your business accounts if you are self-employed, but they would not get very far with just these items. They have the electoral register, so they know who lives where and who pays the rates, and they also have information supplied to them regularly by banks, building societies, auctioneers and other institutions about various transactions. They also receive tip-offs, although the Inland Revenue do not always take these very seriously because they can be (and sometimes are) wholly malicious, but they can lead to other areas of enquiry which the Inland Revenue can find profitable. They also use their initiative. A long-term favourite is for the Inland Revenue to note the numbers of expensive cars and to check up on the registered owner. If the registered owner does not show the car in his books or his declared income is inconsistent with being able to afford such a car, the taxman will be after him. Do not forget that they also receive tax returns and accounts from every other taxpayer, and their enquiries on other people's affairs can lead them to you – or at least provide information which can lead them to check up on you.

If you are moonlighting, it certainly does not pay to advertise because the Inland Revenue read the adverts too. You could perhaps claim that advertising to the world at large could be regarding as 'Notification of a source of income' to the Inland Revenue within the meaning of Section 7, Taxes Management Act 1970, but I doubt it. The lengths that the Inland Revenue will go to in this area is quite surprising. I remember on one occasion discussing a client's tax affairs with the Inspector of Taxes when he produced a press advertisement from his file which set out the number of domestic staff engaged at the client's home. The advertisement was completely anonymous and could only have been traced to my client by a good deal of investigative work by the Inland Revenue. This was somewhat of a shock, and although there was a perfectly reasonable explanation it was a clear lesson about how far the Inland Revenue go in collecting information about particular taxpayers. Had the client been anything less than scrupulous in dealing with his tax affairs he would probably have sunk without trace.

Some people, however, really ask for trouble – and the Inland Revenue are always there to give it to them. How often have you seen a newspaper article or TV interview about a burglary where the victim tells of all the valuable furs and jewellery and paintings which have been stolen. The taxman will always take careful note of the items said to have been stolen and check to see whether they have been notified to him as chargeable assets acquired for capital gains tax purposes – or, indeed, whether the declared income of the individual is such as to enable him to buy such items. If not, an in-depth enquiry into his affairs will assuredly begin.

In a recent case the Inland Revenue clearly could not believe their luck. The taxpayer appeared on a TV programme about his business. Various statements were made about his new Rolls Royce and his other cars, his expensive house, his holiday home and various other matters. Unfortunately he had not sent in tax returns for a number of years and naturally the Inland Revenue went to town.

A similar case arose some time ago regarding a prostitute who was interviewed on the television about her earnings. She should not have been surprised when she received assessments from the Inland Revenue charging tax on the amounts which she said she was earning. What was worse, the VAT man also became interested and she ended up with monumental bills for tax, VAT and a whole host of interest and penalties for non-disclosure and failure to register for VAT.

Whilst on this subject, it is perhaps appropriate to mention that the taxman is not particularly bothered about how income is earned; prostitution is a taxable activity and accounts need to be submitted to the Inland Revenue to show the profits made. Strangely, prostitution is not, contrary to popular belief, a profession – at least not for tax purposes. It is a trade – a matter specifically decided by a recent tax case. Burglary on the other hand is not a trade – not because it is illegal (illegal activities can quite easily be taxable) but because it does not satisfy the definition of a trade for tax purposes.

Inspectors of Taxes are sometimes extremely coy about sexual matters and this can lead them into difficulty – and there is no reason why you should ease their difficulty. If the taxman wants to assess a young lady for prostitution he ought to do so, not hide behind euphemisms such as masseuse, companion, escort or 'teacher: French lessons' unless of course she actually describes herself in that way. An assessment which charges tax as 'masseuse' is simply bad and cannot be enforced if the young lady does not do any massage. If the taxman wants to charge tax for prostitution he must raise an assessment for her as a prostitute and not be squeamish about it. Until he does so there can be no liability.

The Inspectors of Taxes are trained to be vigilant and it is difficult to conduct many activities without coming to their attention. If you run a business, how do you know that the person for whom you do some work is not an Inspector of Taxes or a VAT man? If you carry out work for him, the chances are that he will check that the amount he pays you finds it way into your business accounts – and if you do not have any, some serious questions will be asked. If you make a big play about wanting payment in cash for the work done and are very reluctant to accept a cheque, you may also expect some enquiries to be made.

If you are a musician or market trader you are almost bound to have an Inspector of Taxes in the audience or at your market stall sooner or later, and you are thereby exposed. You can even find yourself playing golf or tennis with an Inspector at the local club and although he is unlikely to use such an opportunity to covertly interrogate you, various personal details will inevitably come out in conversation – where you went on holiday, where your children go to school, and your overall approach to matters of business. And even if you avoid them there is always the risk of being pointed out: 'Oh look, there's John! He is just back from four weeks in the Seychelles.'

I recall one case which involved a solicitor who had back-dated a deed of covenant for a client. He really ought to have known better – see Chapter 9. The Inland Revenue had some reason to doubt the accuracy of the date on the covenant and their suspicions led them to make some enquiries which revealed that the date was wrong. This set off the Inland Revenue equivalent of the fire alarm and the papers quickly found their way to Enquiry Branch. The amount involved was very small, not normally sufficient to excite Enquiry Branch, but the Inland Revenue take the view that if a solicitor or accountant does something dishonest in one case, the likelihood is that they are equally dishonest in relation to all their clients. This is called the 'centre of infection' principle and all the big guns come out because they might be able to discover a whole bundle of taxpayers worthy of investigation. In this case the solicitor involved was 'invited' to attend an interview with the Enquiry Branch who clearly set out to frighten the pants off him. They succeeded. As it turned out, the solicitor was only foolish and ignorant; he had not appreciated the significance of what he had done. However, the real point of this story is that when he was asked whether he had back-dated deeds of covenant before, the solicitor confirmed that he had not, and further stated that he hardly ever drew up deeds of covenant at all. This was viewed with some suspicion by the Inland Revenue who asked how many deeds of covenant he had prepared in the last twelve months. The solicitor thought carefully and said it was probably about three. To his horror the man from Enquiry Branch flicked through his papers and said that was right – and then proceeded to give precise details of those very deeds of covenant. The Inland Revenue had done their homework extremely thoroughly and had dug out all the deeds he had prepared; the fact that they had so much information and had already checked up on the answer to this question was a real lesson to the solicitor. (As a lawyer he ought to have appreciated that Enquiry Branch well know the first lesson in cross-examination – never ask a question unless you know the answer.) The enormity of the consequences of a lie in response to this particular question did not bear thinking about, and this single fact probably had a more significant effect on him than anything else. I doubt whether he will ever transgress again.

## Business Information

The Inland Revenue always find it difficult explaining to their Inspectors of Taxes how various businesses work. Inspectors of Taxes are not businessmen and know nothing of running a business, and that places them at somewhat of a disadvantage. Unless they know something about the particular business and how it works they have no means of judging whether or not the businessman's accounts contain a load of plausible rubbish. One of the modern means of providing Inspectors of Taxes with such information is a series of Business Economic Notes dealing with various business and these are now published by the Inland Revenue. The notes are lengthy and reasonably comprehensive and although they may be criticized as a little too simplistic, concentrating more on how a particular type of business ought to be conducted rather than how it is in fact conducted in real life, they still contain a good deal of useful information. However, it is not the information they contain which is useful but the fact that this information is disseminated to Inspectors of Taxes.

At the time of writing, Business Economic Notes have been published on the following types of business:

Travel Agents
Road Haulage
The Lodging Industry
Hairdressers
Waste Material Reclamation and Disposal
Funeral Directors
Florists
Licensed Victualler
Dentists

Quite what conclusions can be drawn from the choice of these various types of business is difficult to judge, and it would be interesting to see how many more are published and on what further activities. If you are in business in one of these areas it is essential that you obtain a copy of these notes and study the contents. These notes will be used as the basis for the Inland Revenue's enquiry into your accounts and will be used to judge the accuracy and reasonableness of your answers to his enquiries. If your replies are inconsistent with the notes he may well doubt the accuracy of what you say. You would therefore be well advised to draw attention to any areas in the notes which do not precisely fit the particular circumstance of your business because that would avoid the risk of the Inland Revenue taking an adverse and unjustified view about various aspects of your business.

## Gross Profit Percentage

Another fruitful area of Inland Revenue enquiry is gross profit percentages. The Inland Revenue issue GP percentages to tax officers for all sorts of businesses based on the enormous amount of data at their disposal. It goes without saying that all businesses submit accounts to the Inland Revenue and they have an unparalleled amount of information upon which to draw for this information. If you have a retail shop selling widgets and your gross profit is 30 per cent whereas the average GP for all other retail widget sellers is 40 per cent, the Inspector of Taxes will immediately wonder why you are so unprofitable. One reason may be that you are a lousy businessman but another reason may be that some of the takings do not find their way into the business records. This possibility will cause the Inland Revenue to make enquiries and indeed it is quite proper that they should do so in the discharge of their public duty. Some Inspectors of Taxes assume rather too readily that there is obvious wrong-doing and start making all sorts of allegations. As explained in Chapter 9 this should not be a matter of undue concern – unless, of course, you are failing to keep a record of all your business receipts, in which case you should take careful note of the circumstances of Mr Lester Piggott.

If the Inspector of Taxes starts making accusations before he has made any proper enquiries and assumes that you are being dishonest, you should not be too alarmed – if your affairs are going to be investigated it is much better that they should start this way because the Inland Revenue immediately lose the initiative. It is wholly wrong for them to assume without evidence that you are a dishonest person and such prejudice can only act to your advantage (remember the Taxpayers' Charter). Do not react violently; stay calm and get some professional help. It is as likely as not that your professional adviser will be able to explain that there is nothing wrong and that the manner in which the Inland Revenue enquiry started is unjustified. They will be much more ready to back down if they are shown to have acted without grounds or with prejudice than if they behaved reasonably and properly. This is not to say that you should welcome an aggressive and unreasonable approach from the taxman – just that if you get such an approach, do not lose the opportunity for advantage which it immediately presents.

An important point to appreciate about the taxman's gross profit percentage analysis is that it is only an average of other businesses' results. If the widget sellers on average make 40 per cent profit this must mean that some make more than 40 per cent and some make less. If the range is (say) 32–46 per cent and your gross profit is 33 per cent you could reasonably

protest if this is treated as grounds for the suggestion that you
have suppressed your takings. Somebody has to be at the lower
end if the average is to be believed and a moment's thought will
reveal that if all those below 40 per cent are understating
their profits and are really making 40 per cent the average will
go up and up. This mathematical truth often escapes the notice
of the taxman and it is therefore worthwhile bringing it to his
attention fairly early in the correspondence. If you are able
to show some good reason why your particular business is less
profitable than others, you really should not have any difficulty.
Certainly no adverse implications should arise before proper and
detailed enquiries are made.

A very important point about gross profit percentages is that
they are probably only capable of being used as a background
reason for the Inland Revenue starting their enquiries. A suspect gross profit percentage will be enough to make the Inland
Revenue raise an estimated additional assessment to charge you
more tax on the basis that your profits may be understated –
but they may not be able to rely on this data if the dispute
goes to appeal before the Commissioners. At such a hearing,
the Inspector of Taxes will find some difficulty in mentioning
the existence of the average gross profit percentage figures for
the business sector as a whole. Firstly he is bound by the Official
Secrets Act not to reveal details of another taxpayer's affairs,
so if you press him to give an example of another comparable
business with a higher gross profit percentage he will not be
able to do so. Secondly, even if he did so the evidence would be
hearsay and there are very complex rules about the admissibil-
ity of hearsay in appeal proceedings. You will certainly need
professional advice if these points are to be pursued and the
argument may not always be successful, but if the Inspector
of Taxes knows that his case may be severely weakened by
the inadmissible nature of his evidence, it will make him much
more amenable to a negotiated settlement.

If you run a restaurant or provide some other service to the
public, remember that tax officials are members of the public
too and they may well be your customers. It is not unknown
for a restaurant to be visited by a series of Revenue officials
and for them to take full notes of the number of customers,
the type of meals served and all other relevant details, enabling
them to judge the level of your takings on a particular day. If
your accounts when produced do not correspond with the picture

obtained by the Inland Revenue some difficult enquiries may well ensue.

Stories about this sort of problem are legion: one famous case concerns VAT and carrots. The Customs & Excise counted the number of carrots per portion given to customers and calculated how many such portions could be produced from a 5lb tin of carrots. This did not correspond with the details provided by the business and an investigation ensued culminating in some heavy additional assessments to VAT. Much later it was revealed that the Customs & Excise had omitted to take into account the fact that there is quite a lot of fluid in a 5lb tin of carrots. While this is an exceptional episode, it does show that the taxman is quite capable of getting his sums wrong and you should be extremely vigilant to check them all out. Otherwise you will have no reasonable defence when it comes to challenging a demand for extra tax; and remember it is you who have to show that the assessment is wrong, not for the taxman to prove it is right.

*Mortgages*

Mortgages are a rich source of Inland Revenue enquiry and when you think about it, it is so obvious that you wonder how anybody could fail to see the danger. Let us assume that you want to obtain a mortgage to buy a house so you apply to the Building Society or bank for a mortgage on the normal terms – or you perhaps use a mortgage broker to do it for you. In any event you will need to fill in an application form. Mortgages tend to be limited to a multiple of annual income; it varies a great deal depending upon the different mortgage lender and the financial climate prevailing at the time but it would not be unusual to find a Building Society restricting the amount of money they are prepared to lend to you a maximum of 2.5 times your gross annual income. If you want a £75,000 mortgage you therefore needd to have a salary of £30,000 – so what do you do if your salary is only £25,000? What some folk do is to put down on the form that they are earning £30,000. This will not be much good if they are an employee taxed under PAYE because the mortgage lender will immediately write to the employer and discover the truth. However, you may have other income from casual earnings or perhaps dividends or interest received, or you may be self-employed, making it difficult to estimate accurately you current income. These could be some of the factors behind the income figures which you put on the form to support the mortgage application.

The taxman is fairly interested in all this because he knows that repaying a mortgage is difficult – he probably has one himself. He will also have tables showing the monthly repayments for mortgages of all shapes and sizes. He is therefore able to make a judgement about whether he thinks you can afford the mortgage repayments. You may well say that it has nothing to do with him if your mortgage repayments are a struggle – if you are trying to scrimp and save to pay the mortgage the last thing you want is the taxman breathing down your neck. However, if the mortgage seems to be beyond your means the taxman might think that you could have some additional undisclosed and untaxed income which enables you to meet your living expenses.

Obviously, if you were moonlighting and had some spare cash you could always use it to buy food and clothing which would never be discovered by the taxman. At least individual items could not be traced, but if upon investigation it seems that none of your income was used to buy food or clothes, there is an obvious question to be answered. The taxman has no automatic right to see your bank statements but he can usually get round this by obtaining an order from the Commissioners for their production, and they may well reveal suspicious discrepancies. If for example all your salary goes into your bank account and the only debits are specific cheques and your mortgage repayments but no cash withdrawals, the taxman is going to wonder how you get hold of cash for small everyday items. If he has any doubts about anything, he will start to make lots and lots of enquiries.

The first thing he will do is to check whether the size of the mortgage obtained from the bank or Building Society looks consistent with your income. If, taking the figures illustrated above, you have told him that your income is £25,000 but the building society has lent you £75,000, he can do the sums pretty easily. Building Societies tend to be fairly conservative institutions and do not dole out money irresponsibly so if the current formula is 2.5 times your income, on these figures you would have obtained a mortgage of £12,500 more than your income would normally allow. How did you persuade the Building Society to grant you this extra amount? He will immediately ask to see a copy of the mortgage application form. This will show the details of income and if those details match those on your tax return the Inspector of Taxes will almost certainly be satisfied that there is nothing worth pursuing here. However, if the form showed income of £30,000 and he only knows about income of £25,000 he will want to know why. If there is a good explanation (e.g. you have just got a new job at £30,000 a year) then there will be no difficulty but if the figures on the form are not entirely accurate, your problems are about to start.

There are really only two alternatives – either the figures on the form are true or they are not. If the figures are true then there is another £5,000 of income about which the taxman was not aware and he is going to want to know all about it – where did it come from, who pays it to you, what for, when did it start etc. so he can tax it – and if necessary go back to earlier years and tax those years as well – plus of course interest and penalties.

These consequences are likely to be extremely expensive and you may feel that it is better to say that the figure was wrong; there is no further income and the form was only filled in to help get the mortgage. (It is not worthwhile to suggest that you filled the form in by mistake – that is the least believable answer.)

Unfortunately, however, this is unlikely to make any difference – or at least any improvement. Just look at what you are admitting. 'I wanted a mortgage of £75,000 and I knew that if I told the Building Society the truth about my income I would not get the mortgage I wanted. So I deliberately made a false statement about my income on the application form so that the Building Society would be deceived into giving me a larger mortgage than they would otherwise have done.'

At the very least it is strongly arguable that this represents a crime – the most obvious candidate being obtaining property by deception under Section 15 of the Theft Act 1968, an offence which carried a maximum prison sentence of 10 years. Are you really going to admit to that? It is unlikely that a criminal prosecution would ensue, but why should the Inland Revenue think that you are being any more honest with them than with the Building Society? This is all they need to investigate every aspect of your tax affairs going back to the year dot. Also if you say that you only put the high income figure on the form to get the higher mortgage and that you did not have any additional income, the Inland Revenue will probably tax you on it anyway because they will not believe you. This is called jumping out of the frying pan on to the plate so that the taxman can have you for breakfast.

If you are expecting some guidance about what you should do when you find yourself with this awful dilemma, I am afraid you are going to be disappointed. It is too late – the die was cast irrevocably when the signed mortgage application form was sent to the Building Society. All you can do, if you know that you have done this, is to make absolutely sure that your tax affairs are otherwise squeaky clean and that the taxman has no reason at all to doubt the accuracy of any of the details you have provided to him. With luck your foolishness will never be discovered but if it is you will have to suffer the consequences and long negotiations will be necessary if you are to avoid a serious penalty.

## Farmers

Farmers are subject to some special rules but they still get looked at very closely by the taxman. The Inland Revenue issued some helpful notes to accountants in 1988 setting out the results of a review they had undertaken of farm accounts. The notes explain the nature and extent of errors commonly found in farm accounts – furthermore they reveal the taxman's views on such matters as the correct basis of valuation for harvested crops and tenants' rights. The review concentrated on the Newark area but there is no reason to suppose that it is not representative of farms as a whole. Every farmer ought to obtain a copy of these notes from his tax office so that (just like the Business Economic Notes referred to above) he knows exactly what the taxman will be looking for in his accounts, and can correct any obvious errors at an early stage rather than leaving it to the taxman to make adjustments. If you do leave it to him you never know where he will stop.

## Death

Death is an occasion of some significance for the taxman, because it presents him with a very useful opportunity to seek further taxes. It is an occasion of charge for Inheritance Tax and is therefore a time when all the assets of the deceased have to be ascertained and valued. Even if there is no tax involved, perhaps because the whole estate passes to the surviving spouse, the executors still need to know what assets are to pass to the survivor. It is undoubtedly true that many secrets die with the deceased and answers to some questions may therefore be lost forever, but death also exposes some secrets which may well have been successfully hidden during someone's life. For example, it may be discovered that the deceased had bank accounts of which nobody had previously been aware, perhaps containing amounts which could not be reasonably explained by his normal income and savings. There may be items in the house – pictures, paintings, furniture – of substantial value, greater than the taxman might have expected from the deceased's other resources. The taxman will collect all this information and will draw the most disadvantageous conclusions; he will not be put off by the fact that the person who can provide the explanation is dead. If you are faced with such a situation you are in some difficulty, because if the deceased is found to have substantial assets which are inconsistent with his tax returns, it is a bit like being caught holding the smoking gun. There may be a perfectly reasonable explanation of course, but unless it is found and put forward quickly, an adverse inference is irresistible.

In these circumstances it goes without saying that you must find some good reasons how and why the assets came into the possession of the deceased because if you do not the Inspector of Taxes is going to assume that all the value unaccounted for is income which has previously been concealed and should have been charged to tax; he will of course immediately set about assessing and collecting the tax and will also levy interest and penalties. The cost of this to a widow could be enormous so you have to find a way of discouraging the Inspector of Taxes from pursuing this line – you may not succeed completely but every little will help. A discussion with the widow may be a good way to identify a number of possible explanations for the existence of the additional assets – gifts, inheritance, good bargains etc or anything else which might occur to you having regard to the personal circumstances of the deceased. After all, you cannot now question the deceased and you must make some suppositions. The taxman will be making adverse suppositions so there is no reason why you should not make favourable suppositions.

If all these suggestions are disregarded by the Inland Revenue you should make a great play of the fact that the deceased is being accused of wrongdoing and is not able to defend himself. It is very easy to make allegations about somebody when they cannot answer back particularly when you have all the resources of the State behind you. Furthermore, you can reasonably claim that the distress caused to the widow by these suggestions is so great that they ought not to be made unless they are fully justified. The Inland Revenue do react to being told that they are acting unfairly particularly if a prima facie case can be put forward. Often they will go to great lengths to show that they are being fair and are only doing their public duty without fear or favour and pursuing matters which they have a duty to enquire into. You should put them to the trouble of explaining their position, not only because it will concentrate their minds on the relevant points, but also because it will add a great deal to the time and length of the correspondence about which you can complain later.

Another important point concerns costs, and again the Inland Revenue are well aware of the frequent criticism that Inspectors of Taxes force settlements out of taxpayers not because they have done anything wrong but because it is cheaper to pay the tax than to pay an accountant to continue the correspondence. This is not always the case but it is certainly true in enough cases for the matter to be a source of embarrassment (and therefore high sensitivity) within the Inland Revenue, particularly in the case of a deceased taxpayer where it is the widow who will inevitably have to foot the bill.

It does not take much imagination to see the opportunity here. The widow will be in a state of distress and at this very time the Inland Revenue come along and make all sorts of accusations about her husband's integrity, with a view to depriving her of a considerable amount of money which she can ill afford. Is it likely that she will be able to stand up to these allegations, or is she more likely to give in and pay the money just to get the matter out of the way? Providing you can shield the widow from the distressing correspondence it is no bad thing to carry it on at length – giving the taxman every opportunity to demonstrate his insensitivity. The Inspector may well go a long way past the point at which his superiors would agree is reasonable – after all they do not want to be regarded as cold and callous.

You can really go to town here because the outrage that you can express at their pursuit of the widow (which necessarily involves casting aspersions on the integrity of the recently departed) knows no bounds. If you can wrap up some reasonable explanation for the unexplained increase in wealth (or other irregularity) with some forceful indignation you have a real chance of getting the taxman to agree to a compromise. He does not want to be accused of chasing recently bereaved widows and the worse he can be made to feel about doing so, the better.

However, you must take care not to overdo it. If there is really no reasonable explanation your protestations will have a distinctly hollow ring and will not be taken seriously. It is not enough to say a few well chosen words – you are trying to achieve something. If some penalty is inevitable you should work out the best compromise that you can think of, and develop a plan for the ensuing correspondence – before you even start discussing it with the taxman. Even if you have no answers at all, you will always be able to put forward doubts and uncertainties about the possible source of unexplained funds and to claim that the benefit of all available doubts should be given to the deceased. You may end up having to pay some tax but the more doubts you can put forward (always of course making passing references to the increasing cost of professional advice, and frequent references to the bereavement) the lower the ultimate tax is likely to be.

*Fraudulent Assertions*

If your accounts are challenged on the grounds that the Inland Revenue thinks that you have understated your profits and you know that you have not done so, you must play your cards very carefully. If the Inspector of Taxes alleges neglect on your part the onus is upon you to show that you have not been neglectful. It is very difficult to prove a negative. If, however, you are confident that everything is in order and that there is nothing to suggest otherwise, it is highly worthwhile to manoeuvre the Inspector of Taxes into a position where he has no alternative but to suggest that you have deliberately concealed takings or otherwise understated your profits. Do not be alarmed at this course of events because if he can be persuaded to allege fraud you immediately take the initiative. You may for example be able to show that your takings are carefully recorded and the only means of understating the takings is that you have deliberately pocketed some cash. Take him along this road and try to get him to say that this is what he believes. Why is this important? It is important because if the Inspector's case is that you have conducted your business in a deliberately dishonest manner this is not neglect; it is fraud. If he alleges fraud he must prove it. He does not have to prove neglect; the onus is upon you to disprove neglect – but with fraud the onus is wholly upon him and it makes his job enormously difficult. Indeed it (probably) makes his job too difficult and he will want to wriggle out of it the moment he realizes the problem he faces. However, if your negotiations have been skilfully conducted he will have a great deal of difficulty back-tracking because you will have closed all his available doors as you went along. This will place you in a very strong position to conclude the matter favourably.

## Back-dating Documents

There seems to be a general lack of awareness about the seriousness of back-dating a document – a letter, a claim for relief, a company resolution for the payment of a dividend, or anything. If you back-date a document it is generally for a purpose, usually that you want to make it look as if something happened at an earlier date when you know that it did not. This is not a matter of tax law but falls within the law relating to forgery and is governed by the Forgery and Counterfeiting Act 1981 (although it is likely also to involve the common law offence of Cheating Her Majesty's Revenue). A person is guilty of the offence of forgery if he makes a false instrument with the intention that he or another shall use it to induce a third party to accept it as genuine so that they will do something (or not do something) to their own or another person's prejudice.

The definition of what is a false instrument is rather wide and includes a document which purports to be made:

a)  In a particular form or manner.
b)  With somebody's authority.
c)  At a particular date.
d)  By a particular person when it was not so made.

So if you back-date a document it is just as much a forgery as if you forged somebody's signature to a document and the criminal consequences are the same. It carries a prison sentence. It is no good to say that it does not matter -- the back-dated document only does what you wanted to do anyway if you had got round to doing it at the time. The only reasonable defence in these circumstances is that you are not intending to represent the date as a material fact and that the date would not induce action to anybody's prejudice. However, if the date on the document is not material, what is the point of back-dating it in the first place? The message is clear: if you want to back-date something you probably have a reason and that will almost certainly mean that you should not do so – at least not without running a considerable risk of criminal prosecution.

An example is the case of R v. Patel which contained more than a little irony. In 1965 when Corporation Tax was introduced Mr Patel thought he would take advantage of some relieving provisions by the payment of a dividend before 6th April 1965. Unfortunately he only decided to do so sometime later so he dated the dividend resolution prior to 6th April 1965. In the fullness of time this was revealed as a forgery and he ended up with a suspended prison sentence. The irony was that because he did not fully understand the tax rules, even if he had declared the dividend on the date stated, it would not have saved him any tax anyway.

The consequences of a criminal prosecution may be wider than at first imagined, particularly for a professional person. Quite apart from the fact that he could go to prison or incur a heavy fine it is likely to deprive the professional man of his livelihood – either because the relevant professional body will decide he is not a fit and proper person to continue as a member of that body, or because if he is involved with tax matters he can hardly expect the Inland Revenue ever to believe what he says again. There is also Section 99 TMA 1970 which enables the Inland Revenue to have free access to all the confidential papers relating to his clients. Such a person is therefore unlikely to keep any clients when they discover that all their confidential papers have become freely available to the Inland Revenue.

*Chapter Eight*

# COMMON
# MISUNDERSTANDINGS,
# ERRORS AND QUIRKS

# COMMON MISUNDERSTANDINGS

There are so many old wives' tales about taxation that it would take an encyclopaedia to deal with them all and I can only pick a few areas which seem to be worth exposing. These misunderstandings may arise from casual conversations and can cause an immense amount of damage, so this chapter is intended to go some way to protecting those who conduct their tax affairs on the basis of bar-room gossip.

The various notions that the taxman will never know, or that he will not be able to prove anything, may already have taken a knock in earlier chapters, but here we are concerned with areas where there exists a widespread misunderstanding of the rules.

## Offshore Income

The biggest genus of misunderstanding relates to having money offshore and how this affect your tax liability. There are a surprising number of people who think that simply putting your money offshore, or being paid your salary abroad, somehow means it is not taxable.

Would that it were that easy! Well perhaps not, or those who have taken the trouble to learn all about tax and make their living from such knowledge would be out of a job.

What is so strange about this point of view is that it is so obviously absurd. Can any sensible person really think that if he puts his money in his Barcloyds deposit account in England, the interest will be taxable, but if he puts it in a deposit account at Barcloyds Jersey, it will somehow escape tax? Whatever you may think of the Inland Revenue or of the particular Government in office at the time, they would have to be a bit simple to leave such an enormous opportunity open. It is surely much more likely that this particular idea had been thought of rather a long time ago and the rules designed to make sure it didn't work.

For most people it does not matter where they have their investments, in England, the Cayman Islands or anywhere else. All the income arising will be fully taxable in the UK and so will any capital gains which are made on the investments. Whilst this is true as a general principle, the position can be made more complicated and therefore lead to confusion if for example you are not domiciled in the UK. (For further details on this subject see Chapter 5.) Individuals not domiciled in the UK are still within the scope of Income Tax and Capital Gains Tax but there is a particular relief applicable to them – which is that income arising abroad and gains made on the assets situated abroad will only be actually chargeable to tax when the money is directly or indirectly brought to this country. This is the central theme for many tax-saving techniques with foreign domiciled individuals but expert advice is absolutely necessary. Indeed, the rules are so complex, being designed to prevent people getting an advantage in this way, that it is quite possible (and not unusual) for you to end up with a substantially increased tax liability.

A well known example concerned a Mr Brackett who set up a company in Jersey, through which he intended to operate his business. The idea was simple enough; Mr Brackett would work for the Jersey company and be paid a modest salary but all the income from his work in the UK would be paid into the Jersey company where it would be free of Jersey tax.

He was right that it would not give rise to any Jersey tax but unfortunately the plan stood little chance of saving UK tax; indeed quite the reverse. The tax rules were more than sufficient to allow the taxman to charge Mr Brackett to tax personally on the whole of the company's income. Furthermore there was no good reason why his salary should not continue to be taxed even though it derived from the same income – and to make matters worse the company could be charged to corporation tax as well.

So remember the general principle that unless there is something special about your personal circumstances (in which case you must take professional advice) it does not matter where you put your money, or even whether you are paid abroad. Foreign income arising to a UK resident and domiciled person is chargeable to UK tax and having it invested, or paid to an account in Liberia, Bermuda or elsewhere will not make any difference.

## Date of Disposal of Assets

When you dispose of an asset, whether it is part of your trading stock, or whether it is a capital asset giving rise to capital gain, the date of disposal is always the date of the contract. This is the date of sale and *not* the date of transfer or completion. The most obvious example is the sale of a house. Usually there is an exchange of contracts with completion taking place some time later. The date of completion is entirely irrelevant for tax purposes – it is always the date when the contracts are exchanged which is the important date. In the case of shares the relevant date is usually the date on the share transfer form or some other documentation – not the date when the share certificate is issued. This can be extremely important when a sale takes place around 5th April. Many people have arranged to defer completion of a sale until after 5th April, thinking the Capital Gains Tax will fall in the next year; if you can defer the date of sale until the following tax year you do not have to pay the tax for a further twelve months. For example if you exchange contracts on 1st March 1990 and arrange for completion to take place on 10th April 1990 you might think that you can claim that the sale took place on 10th April, that is in the tax year 1990/91, so that the tax is not payable until 1 December 1991. This is entirely wrong and can be very expensive. In this illustration the sale took place on 1 March 1990, in the tax year 1989/90 and the tax is payable on 1 December 1990. If you put the disposal on the wrong tax return you are very likely to find that the Inland Revenue will charge you interest (at least) from the date when the tax should have been paid and not when they find out about it.

One important exception to this principle concerns conditional contracts although it is not really an exception because a conditional contract is not a contract at all; it is something which will blossom into a contract when the condition is satisfied. Where there is a conditional contract e.g. a sale of a house on condition that planning permission is obtained, it will become a sale (and therefore a disposal for Capital Gains Tax purposes) when the condition is fulfilled.

On this subject the taxman is not above putting forward the most highly technical arguments if he can see that it might give him an opportunity to charge some tax. An example might be the position of a person who is intending to leave the UK permanently but who would like to tidy up his affairs before his departure including disposing of those assets which he no longer requires. He may have a valuable property but he would know from Chapter 5 that if he sells it before he leaves he will be liable to Capital Gains Tax. So he decides to sell it after his departure, or preferably in the subsequent tax year so that he is completely safe.

In these circumstances the taxman has been known to argue that the sale actually took place before the departure and that only the transfer formalities were dealt with later. You might draw attention to the fact that various provisions in the Law of Property Act 1925 require contracts for the sale of land to be in writing, but the taxman will respond that the existence of writing only makes the pre-existing contract enforceable by the purchaser; even without the writing there was still a contract and therefore a disposal for CGT purposes. Whatever one may think about this as an argument it is obviously better to avoid the problem if possible; one way of doing so is to make the contract conditional upon some event or circumstance that can only be satisfied after the vendor's departure. Even if the taxman pursues this argument the special rule relating to conditional contracts will mean that the date of disposal cannot occur until after departure.

## Tax Relief for Interest Paid

It is often thought that if you borrow up to £30,000 secured on your house you will get tax relief for the borrowing. After all, interest on borrowings up to that limit is available for loans to buy owner-occupied property. However, a moment's thought will tell you that it is what you do with the money borrowed and not what it is secured on which really matters. You must look at how you spend the money. If it is to assist you in buying your main residence or to replace borrowings which were themselves used to buy the house, relief will be available, but if you use the money to buy a car or a boat or even do improvements to your house it will not be eligible for a tax deduction.

## Composite Rate Tax

There is a widespread assumption, which is fostered by numerous advertisements for all sorts of investment 'opportunities', that income which has tax deducted at source is tax free in the hands of the investor. This misunderstanding is particularly acute in the case of Building Society interest and bank deposit interest which is paid net of a special rate of tax known as the composite rate. It is an error, sometimes a serious error, to think of such an income as tax free because although for some people the amount they actually receive is subject to no further tax, for others this is not the case.

The system of composite rate tax is rather like PAYE – the tax is deducted before you receive the money (but you would hardly describe your salary as tax free for that reason). The composite rate tax which you are treated as having paid at source on your investment income is effectively equal to the basic rate of tax so that if you are not liable to tax at the higher rate there is no further tax to pay. However, there are important differences which can come as a surprise to the investor. Unlike PAYE, composite rate tax only covers the basic rate so if you are liable to tax at the higher rate you will receive a demand for more tax later in the year.

There is a further implication here because if you regard such income as 'tax free' and do not tell the taxman about it (after all you do not have to tell the taxman about the tax free profits on national savings certificates or yearly plans for example) you will be in default and the taxman will be after you for interest and penalties for failure to show it on your tax return. He may even use it as an excuse to enquire further into your tax affairs and put you to a lot of unnecessary trouble – simply because of your misunderstanding about the nature of this income.

At the other end of the scale you may not be liable to income tax on the whole of the income anyway (because you may have allowances or charges to set against it) but you cannot get a refund of the composite rate tax which you are deemed to have paid at source. This means that you could end up receiving a good deal less by way of net income than if you invested your money in something else. If these circumstances are likely to arise you will be much better off putting your money into the National Savings Bank or into a National Savings Income Bond which pays a high rate of interest without deduction of tax at source.

*Private Residence Exemption*

There seems to be a widespread tendency to think that if you have more than one house you can tell the taxman that you live in one and not the other so that you can obtain the private residence exemption from Capital Gains Tax as you please. Like many misunderstandings it is based on an underlying truth, but it ends up being confused and distorted beyond recognition. There are some very strict rules. If you have a house in which you have lived throughout your period of ownership, it will be exempt from Capital Gains Tax when you sell it; if you want to move but you cannot sell your old house before moving into the new house do not worry – the rules allow you two years in which to sell the old house without prejudicing your Capital Gains Tax exemption. So for that two-year period you can effectively have two houses which are exempt from Capital Gains Tax. Apart from this, you generally cannot get the private residence exemption in respect of more than one house for the same period – and you are only entitled to the exemption for the periods in which you live in the house as your only or main residence. So you cannot move from one house to another and expect to have Capital Gains Tax exemption on both houses unless throughout your period of ownership of both houses they were your only or main residences. If they were not, the exemption will be scaled down for the periods in which you actually lived in each house.

If you live in one house and acquire another place of residence (it need only be a rented flat because all that is required is an interest in the property; a leasehold interest will be quite sufficient) you can make a claim to the Inland Revenue to treat one property (and one only) as your main residence for the purposes of the exemption. You have two years in which to make the election and if you fail to do so the property qualifying for the exemption will be the one which is used the most for your residential purposes. But remember this election does not apply to any old property but only to properties which are actually used by you as a residence.It is no good saying that you will tell the taxman where you lived and he will not be able to prove you wrong. You will remember that he does not have to do so. If he has any reason to think that your account of your residential movements is wrong he will simply raise an assessment to charge tax on the capital gain and you will have the burden of proving that the assessment is wrong.

## Gifts

It is a mistake to think that gifts are somehow outside the scope of taxation. The only tax which is not going to apply to a gift is Stamp Duty. VAT can apply and so can Income Tax, Capital Gains Tax and Inheritance Tax.

As far as Income Tax is concerned a gift will be chargeable to Income Tax in the hands of the recipient if it arises from the employment (if you are employed) or arises out of the trade (if you are self-employed). The important factor is whether you receive the gift by virtue of the fact that you are an employee or as part of your business. A taxi driver's tips are taxable and so are tips to restaurant staff and even an Easter offering to a clergyman. It does not matter who gives you the gift or whether it is in money. If you receive value and you would not have received it had you not been an employee, or a trader, it will be taxable. This may seem harsh but that is the rule. To avoid tax on a gift you have to show that it was received by you by virtue of your personal qualities and nothing to do with your job. It may be that your job gave you the opportunity to show that you had these fine personal qualities deserving of a gratuity but that is not enough to make it taxable. This is extremely difficult to prove and the taxman will always assume that gifts are taxable, so if you do receive a gift or are likely to receive one, make sure that the reason for the gift can be proved to be nothing to do with the job or the services you perform.

For Capital Gains Tax purposes a gift of something is nearly always treated as if it had been a sale by the donor at market value. Certain types of asset are exempt from Capital Gains Tax (such as motor cars) but that does not mean that they are not treated as disposals at market value, so if you are contemplating making a gift you should seek professional advice so that your generosity does not prove counter-productive by creating a tax liability – plus interest and penalties if the gift is not discovered by, or reported to, the Inland Revenue until some time later.

Inheritance Tax is specifically designed to tax gifts although these days a gift from one individual to another does not give rise to any tax unless the donor dies within seven years of making the gift. Unfortunately the Inheritance Tax rules are immensely complex and nobody should contemplate making gifts with a view to saving Inheritance Tax without professional advice. If you are not careful (and sometimes even if you are) you can end up paying a lot more tax than if you had done nothing at all.

One client of mine had the bright idea that if he gave an employee of his company gifts instead of salary the employee would not pay tax on the money and that would be a good way of saving some tax. This was rather misconceived because what happened is that the Inland Revenue suggested (quite rightly) that the employee received the gifts by virtue of the fact that he was an employee and he should have paid tax on them. However, it was the client and not the company who made the gifts so that no tax deduction was available for the amounts involved. (The reasoning here is that it was the company that was carrying on the trade but the company did not make the gifts; the shareholder made the gifts but he was not carrying on a trade from which he could seek a tax deduction.) The client therefore paid out his own money (on which he had already paid tax) to the employee who paid some more tax on the gifts, so additional tax was therefore created out of thin air. If the company had just increased their employee's salary everything would have been fine. To make matters worse, the Inland Revenue decided to start a full investigation into the employee's affairs because he had clearly more to live on than could be explained by his salary from the company. The Inland Revenue could not believe that anybody could be so foolish as to do this innocently and went looking really hard for something sinister; the whole episode turned into a disaster.

## Residence

The concept of residence is explained in some detail in Chapter 4 but one common misunderstanding ought to be explained here. You do not avoid UK tax by simply being out of the country for a whole tax year. It is possible that if you take up a settled residence abroad for a whole tax year, for a specific purpose, you could be regarded as not resident for that year in which case you may be able to avoid Income Tax on some of your income, but the taxman may well claim that you were absent from the UK only for the purposes of occasional residence abroad and that you should therefore be treated as resident in the UK throughout the period. He has powerful authority for this argument. The concept of 'occasional residence' is a difficult one and need not be examined in detail here because anybody taking such a drastic step as going abroad for a whole tax year should never do so without taking proper professional advice. In any event income arising in the UK generally remains chargeable to Income Tax even if you can establish non-residence; Capital Gains Tax is, of course, entirely unaffected. Capital Gains Tax liability is determined by ordinary residence which requires at the very least an absence from the UK for three complete tax years. As far as Inheritance Tax is concerned becoming non-resident is a complete waste of time because Inheritance Tax is not chargeable by reference to residence at all – it is determined by reference to domicile.

## Delaying Payment of Tax as Long as Possible

The idea that you should try to delay paying your tax as long as you possibly can has roots going back centuries and before 1975 there was a great deal that could be done to delay the payment of tax to your advantage. You can still delay the payment of your tax, sometimes for many years, but there is a severe sting in the tail. In 1975 the Inland Revenue revised the rules relating to interest on unpaid tax and there emerged the concept of a 'reckonable date' which is the date from which interest starts to run if you have not paid your tax; in 1986 this was considerably strengthened.

There are two main ways in which you can delay payment of your tax. You can avoid telling the taxman about your income so that he does not raise an assessment or if an assessment has been raised, persuade the taxman that you have been overcharged and obtain 'postponement' of the tax assessed. This will mean that the tax does not actually become payable until the liability is finally agreed with the taxman and that could take many years. However, both the above overlook the interest implications. If you just fail to tell the taxman about your income he will assuredly charge you interest (and a hefty penalty) when he finally finds out about it. This will be charged from the date when you should have paid the tax and as will be seen from Chapter 10 this can be very expensive indeed because the interest rate is fairly high and there is no tax deduction allowed for such interest. If you are in business and you had increased your overdraft to pay the tax, the overdraft interest will be tax deductible. Furthermore, penalties are mainly tax related, that is to say based on the amount of the tax and any deliberate concealment of income is likely to give rise to a substantial penalty.

If you postpone the tax on an assessment issued by the taxman, interest will run from, at the latest, six months after the date when the tax ought to have been paid. Sometimes, for example if you are not going to get a tax deduction for any interest paid if you borrow the money to pay the tax, you might regard the Inland Revenue as an acceptable source of credit but they are aware of this possibility and will be very careful before they accept your postponement application.

Neither does it help if the taxman underestimates your income and raises an assessment which is inadequate, because since 1987 this will not save you from interest on the amount of tax you should have paid if the income had been assessed correctly – and which will be assessed later when the true figures are known. You may feel that this is rather a strict regime, and so it is, but it derives from an increasing drive within the Inland Revenue to ensure that everybody pays their tax promptly, which in principle can hardly be a matter of complaint.

*Common Errors*

It is well worth repeating that the Inland Revenue have a unique and comprehensive information source which is available only to them, i.e. the details of everybody's tax return and the way in which they deal with their tax affairs. This includes the work of accountants and tax advisers who prepare accounts and send them in to the Inland Revenue for the purpose of agreeing tax liabilities. Naturally, with the best will in the world errors will be made and this information enables the Inland Revenue to analyse the errors, to identify various areas where errors are more likely and to concentrate on the areas deserving of special attention. So if you or your adviser do not want to become involved in lengthly correspondence with the Inland Revenue, it is worth paying special attention to those areas which the taxman will probably be looking at. The Inland Revenue recently produced a list of the most frequent errors, in the expectation, it is assumed, that their workload would be reduced if people made sure that these things were right before sending details into the Inland Revenue. This works both ways because if you can identify an error before the Inland Revenue does, there is a good chance that you will escape the consequences of interest and penalties for non-disclosure or underpayment of taxes. The list provided by the Inland Revenue includes the following:

a) Arithmetical errors. This is so blindingly obvious that it barely needs mentioning but it is as well to check the arithmetic of anything you send to the taxman – he will. He will not be impressed if he finds errors in your arithmetic because he may well consider that there are other errors elsewhere which he has not yet discovered. One particular source of confusion is the use of brackets to show a negative figure such as a loss, but if you subtract a negative it means that you add it on, and if you add a negative it means that you deduct it. It is not difficult to see that this can easily lead to errors. The taxman tends to be rather cynical about arithmetical errors because they have an unerring tendency to be in the taxpayer's favour.

b) Claiming a tax deduction for expenses which are not allowable. This is a real favourite because many people try to claim such items and the taxman is always alert to find items claimed which are not properly allowable. Entertaining expenses are never deductible nor are travelling expenses from home to work and if you claim these you are either ignorant or trying it on. Either way he will not view the details you send him with much respect and you can expect him to go through everything in detail to see whether any other errors may have been made. This is not to say you should err on the taxman's side by failing to claim doubtful items. By all means claim every conceivable item of expenditure but do so in a way which does not give rise to any adverse implications; for example if you are claiming travelling expenses which are *prima facie* disallowable, give him some explanation why you feel they are allowable. This will at least show him that you are not trying to sneak an advantage hoping that he will not notice. You need to avoid damaging your own credibility. If you are in doubt as to the technical position you can take professional advice, or look the item up in many of the do-it-yourself guides to taxation. Or you could just write and explain why you think that you should have a tax deduction for the particular item. If he writes back and says that there is no deduction available, do not accept it blindly even if he quotes impressive authority against you. This point is examined in more detail in Chapter 8.

c) Confusing the distinction between capital expenditure and revenue expenditure. It is hardly surprising that this gives rise to errors because even the House of Lords has said that the matter is so uncertain and the tests so difficult to synthesise that the answer may just as well be obtained by flicking a coin. Capital expenditure is not tax deductible (although you can claim an allowance in respect of some capital expenditure) whereas revenue expenditure is tax deductible. It is no surprise that many people like to treat capital expenditure as revenue expenditure for this very reason. Unfortunately the distinction is one of the most complex matters known to tax law and there will be masses of conflicting authority to support either the taxman's view that the expenditure is capital or your view that it is not. You will not win this argument (if at all) without professional advice so you need to consider whether the amounts involved are worth it.

d) Income or expenditure being attributed to the wrong year. Obviously this will have an effect on your tax liability for a particular year and the taxman will therefore make it his business to check whether the figures are right. You should check it first and put any errors right if only to avoid unnecessary exchanges of correspondence with the taxman.

e) Capital gains not reported. This is a real problem for the taxman because he will rarely if ever have details of capital gains early enough to enable him to raise an assessment in time for you to pay the tax on the due date. You will need to tell him. He will know that you have income and will assume that you have the same income as last year if it is normally of a recurring character; he can therefore raise an assessment on an estimated basis to collect some tax even if he does not have the precise details. However, capital gains are not inevitably recurring and he has no reason to raise an assessment For this reason the taxman treats failure to provide details of capital gains at the right time as a serious matter and will inevitably charge interest and penalties for failure to report capital gains. The amounts involved tend to be quite high and the penalties will therefore be significant. So, if you want to avoid trouble and expense (and possible further difficulty by his extending his enquiry into your affairs still further) you should make quite sure that you do not over-look any capital gains – and be careful to let him know by the 31 October after the end of the tax year in which the gains were made. This is dealt with in more detail in Chapter 15.

f) The remainder of the items which the taxman puts on his list are of a fairly technical nature, e.g.

incorrect claims in respect of losses
miscalculation of small companies relief
miscalculation of capital allowance computations
claiming of charges accrued and not paid

but these tend to be more matters for the professional adviser.

You should also be aware that the taxman will always reconcile the fixed asset figures shown in a set of accounts with the figures shown on your capital allowances claim. If you are sensible you will do this before sending the accounts to the taxman. It is surprising just how many times a small error arises with these figures and if you allow the taxman to pick it up before you do, you are inviting him to see whether you have been careless in other areas.

## Changing Taxmen

Another favourite ploy if you see the taxman getting a little too close for comfort is to try to change your tax district so that your case gets transferred to another tax inspector. This sounds like a good idea but it does not work anything like as well as you might think. You may actually end up with somebody much worse but that is the risk you take. However, you should always appreciate that even if he is not, Inspectors of Taxes always make lots of notes to go on the file for this successor to see. The new man will naturally want to familiarise himself with the case and will read the file from start to finish with a fresh eye. Is that really what you are after? Unfortunately there is a much more compelling reason why this transfer will not get you out of a difficulty and that is because the taxman works on the 'I've started so I'll finish' principle and will not release his file to the new district until his present enquiries are concluded.

However, although a change will not get you out of a particular problem, it could be worthwhile moving your file to get out of the firing line of a particularly unpleasant taxman. He may never get round to you, and even if he does he may do you no harm, but it may be better to leave than risk the aggravation. But remember that Inspectors of Taxes get transferred too and it could just happen that you are reunited in a new tax district. It does happen – but it would be very bad luck.

Changing your tax office is not altogether an easy matter for individuals and sometimes it is impossible. Companies can do it easily, simply by changing their Registered Office, because this automatically changes the tax office. Individual's tax offices are determined by their employer's address or their home address, and it may be difficult to change either. If you have more than one place of work or more than one home you will have more scope (but do watch out if you are claiming tax relief on your mortgage on the basis that you live in home A, and you suddenly start arguing that you really live at home B). If you work from home you are in some difficulty if you want to change your tax office – you would be much better advised to string out the correspondence and hope that the Inspector of Taxes moves before you do.

## *Expenses Claims*

Perhaps the area of most confusion surrounds the claiming of a tax deduction for expenses. The problem here is that all sorts of expenses are claimed by all sorts of people and they get away with it. The ordinary person does not know whether they got their tax deduction because of some technical argument, or because of some administrative practice of the Inland Revenue, or simply by default. The truth is that the rules for deduction of expenses are so strict that the most usual reason for a tax deduction is because the Inland Revenue take a reasonable view and allow the expense as a sort of concession. It is very important to know because it will affect the way you approach the taxman when arguing for tax relief for expenses. Elsewhere it is explained that courtesy and a professional approach pays dividends because negotiations with the taxman will invariably be required. If you are in business the rule is that the expenses must be 'wholly and exclusively incurred for the purposes of the business'. This leads to a most important principle which is 'duality of purpose'. What this means is that if you incur some expense partly for business reasons and partly for other reasons you do not get part of the expense allowed – you will get none of it. The best example recently is that of Miss Anne Mallalieu, a barrister who was obviously able to argue her case with great skill. She still lost. She claimed the expense of buying and keeping clean the black clothing which she was required to wear in court. The professional code of conduct of barristers require that they wear black clothing in court. She did not like black clothing and wore it only for her work so you would think she had a cast-iron case. Unfortunately, the principle of duality of purpose was her downfall. What the Inland Revenue successfully claimed was that she did not only buy the black clothes for wearing in court – she had another purpose which was that she needed to wear clothes to remain decent. This latter purpose was not a business purpose but was a private purpose and therefore she infringed the duality of purpose rule. You may not like this decision and may think it is daft, but it is the law and if you try to ignore it you are even dafter.

Fortunately, however, the Inland Revenue are very rarely as strict as this in their approach and often, indeed nearly always, allow expenses where they have a clear business purpose – providing there is no other purpose which is too obvious. Even if there is (for example if you fill up your car with petrol which you will use for private purposes as well as business purposes) they will allow a proportion to be tax deductible. But watch out – if you press too hard you must remember that at the end of the day the taxman could simply say the magic words 'duality of purpose' and your claim will go out of the window.

What you must do is consider very carefully your claim for expenses and to be prepared for a challenge. If the duality of purpose argument is raised (or even if it is not) do not be led into making general statements which indicates a dual purpose for the expenditure. Providing the *purpose* of the expenditure was wholly and exclusively business, it does not matter that you derive some personal benefit from it – that will not preclude a tax deduction. What matters is that the expenditure was not actually incurred for the purpose of getting the private benefit as well. If for example you have to go to the South of France during the summer to see a client or otherwise for a *bona fide* business purpose you may as well enjoy yourself on the beach (or in the casino) in your spare time. This does not matter – providing this was not one of your reasons for going; it was just a fortuitous and pleasant side effect. You should not be drawn into admitting that you thought it would be a good place to have a good time as well, because this will prejudice your perfectly proper tax deduction. However, if you take your wife with you it will obviously be much more difficult to say that the trip had an exclusive business purpose – even if you pay the costs of your wife's journey privately. But do not abandon hope even in this circumstance; you may well be able to put forward good reasons why your wife was an essential part of your visit – in some countries being entertained by customers without a female companion is positively detrimental to the business prospect.

If you are employed and you want to claim expenses you have the most difficult task known to taxation. You must understand the precise rule and make your circumstances fit or you will be wasting your time. The rule for employees is that the expenses must be 'wholly exclusively and necessarily incurred in the performance of the duties of the employment'. You should carefully note the difference between this and the self-employed rule where there is no requirement for 'necessity', nor any requirement that the money must have been spent 'in the performance' of the work. One reason why you should carefully note the distinction is because Inspectors of Taxes often mix them up – not completely, but they often lay the wrong emphasis on the tests to your disadvantage. If you can pick up that they are applying the wrong test or a mishmash of tests you are a long way towards winning the argument.

However, back to the strict rule for employees. You may say, with a lot of justification, that if you spend money wholly and exclusively in the performance of your duties and which is necessarily incurred, why on earth did your employer not pay – after all if it is necessary he jolly well ought to pick up the tab. Quite right too – and if he does not, the taxman will say that this proves that it was not necessarily incurred and your claim fails. However, this is not right – it may be evidence but that does not mean it is conclusive. Do not be browbeaten by the Inspector of Taxes into giving up your claim. For example, if your employer does not supply you with overalls or a hard hat, but these are needed for your work and you have to buy them yourself, you are entitled to a tax deduction for them.

## *Winning on the Horses*

One of the favourite reasons given by taxpayers who are in difficulty explaining how they happen to be in possession of substantial sums of money, or assets of a value which they simply could not have acquired from the resources known to the Inland Revenue, is that they won money on the horses. There is a great problem here because whether it is true or false you are still in trouble.

If it is false the consequences are obvious. The taxman will simply refuse to accept the suggestion at all without proof in the form of documentary evidence and if you try and provide false documentary evidence to substantiate your claim you become immediately involved in tax evasion, forgery, attempted theft and numerous other offences let alone the common law offence of Cheating Her Majesty's Revenue. Little more needs to be said about this.

However, the position is not much better even if it is true. You will be able to obtain proof from the betting shop or other organisation that you had a large win and you may feel this is conclusive. Indeed the fact that you had a large win will not be disputed by the Inland Revenue because Ladbrokes or William Hill or whoever certainly would not say that you had such a win unless it was true. However, this proves only that you had a win – what it does not prove is how many bets you had previously placed which did not win – i.e. the amount of your losses. It defies reason to suggest that your one big win came from an isolated bet – it is far more likely that you regularly bet on horses and like all punters, you regularly lose reasonable amounts of money. Indeed the taxman may go on to suggest that your win probably merely recouped your earlier losses – and possibly not even that. Accordingly you are no further forward. If the win money caused you to break even, you must have previously spent an equal amount of money on earlier bets – so where did that money come from? You are back to square one and your ace card, upon which you were probably hoping to rely, has been royally trumped. It is for this reason that saying you had a big win is unlikely to be much use, unless you are really the wholly exceptional case of somebody who never bets, but was persuaded to put some money on a friend's horse as a gesture to the owner or trainer and it came romping home. There is little need to dwell on the consequences of such a lucky win – except to

say that the taxman would still need convincing that you are not
a regular punter. If you are not it should be easy to obtain sworn
statements from your friends saying that you did not regularly
bet on horses, and the person who gave you the opportunity to
win will be able to confirm that you are obviously a novice and
had to be persuaded to part with your money in the first place.

*Interest Paid*

The Inland Revenue sometimes find themselves a hobby horse
and large numbers of Inspectors of Taxes will suddenly all start
asking questions about the same thing. This sounds bad but
it is an immediate problem for the Inland Revenue because a
blanket approach on any subject means they are not considering
your affairs properly – they are obviously prejudging the issue
without knowledge of the facts. They tried such an approach
with freelance journalists and people working in television
some time ago, suggesting that they should not be regarded as
self-employed at all, but as employees, subject to tax deduction
under PAYE. This is a subject all of its own and is covered in
detail in Chapter 14. Another example of an Inland Revenue
hobby horse in recent years is the attempt by Inspectors of Taxes
to disallow overdraft interest as a tax deduction in the accounts
of a sole trader or partnership business where the trader or one
of the partners has become overdrawn on his capital account.
This is a fairly technical point but it is sufficiently widespread
to deserve explanation. A simple balance sheet of a business
would be:

| Mr & Mrs Proprietor: | Capital | 10,000 |
|---|---|---|
| | Profit for year | 8,000 |
| | | 18,000 |
| | drawings | 14,000 |
| | Capital Employed | £4,000 |
| | Business equipment | 5,000 |

|  |  |  |
|---|---|---|
| stock |  | 20,000 |
| debtors |  | 14,000 |
|  |  | 39,000 |
| creditors | 23,000 |  |
| overdraft | 12,000 | 35,000 |
| Total Assets |  | £4,000 |

There is no particular problem here as far as the taxman is concerned. The creditors and the overdraft are a little high and the business is therefore under financial pressure – made worse by the fact that Mr & Mrs Proprietor have drawn £14,000 out of the business when they had made profits of only £8,000. However, as it stands, there is no difficulty. But let us look at two possible alternative positions for the following year:

|  | A | B |
|---|---|---|
| Capital | 4,000 | 4,000 |
| Loss for year | 5,000 | 5,000 |
|  | (1,000) | (1,000) |
| drawings | 6,000 | – |
|  | £(7,000) | £(1,000) |
| Assets | 5,000 | 5,000 |
| Stock | 20,000 | 20,000 |
| debtors | 12,000 | 12,000 |
|  | 37,000 | 37,000 |

| creditors | 27,000 | | 25,000 | |
|---|---|---|---|---|
| overdraft | 17,000 | 44,000 | 13,000 | 38,000 |
| | | £(7,000) | | £(1,000) |

What the taxman will say in the first case is that the Proprietors have drawn out £7,000 more than the business assets and have done so by increasing the bank overdraft. The £7,000 increase in the overdraft was not for business purposes but to allow the Proprietors to draw out more than they were entitled; therefore the interest on the bank overdraft should not be tax deductible. There is some substance in this point because if in either case the Proprietors were now to draw out further amounts for their own use, they are clearly not owed anything by the business – and therefore any increase in the bank overdraft and the consequential overdraft interest to provide the money for them cannot be for the purposes of the business.

However, things are never as simple as that. Look at example B. The proprietors have not drawn out any money so why should the overdrawn partners' account cause any bank interest to be disallowed. It should not – and there should be no argument about it. Look again at example A. He drew out only £6,000 during the year and at the very least that must be the limit of any restriction to the interest relief; however on further examination you will see that the bank overdraft has in fact increased by only £5,000. So why should the taxman restrict relief for the bank overdraft interest beyond the level of the overdraft increase? The answer is that he should not and the fact that Inspectors of Taxes invariably try to do so merely exposes their lack of understanding.

For the taxman to succeed on this argument he must show that the overdraft interest which he wishes to disallow has been caused by the drawings of the Proprietors beyond their entitlement from the business. This is not a matter of accounting theory, it is a matter of cold fact – how much extra overdraft interest has been paid by virtue of this non-business withdrawal. Accordingly, it is necessary to examine the capital side of the balance sheet a little more closely. In both examples the partners' account is overdrawn because of the loss, and it is made worse in example A by further drawings. But just looking at the loss gives a distorted picture. The loss made in the year may or may not have increased the overdraft at all, but even if it had done so you should not necessarily be denied tax relief. It is the fact that the partners have drawn out money beyond their entitlement which has given rise to the increased bank overdraft – or has it?

When the figures of loss for the year are looked into it will be found (or it may be safely assumed) that it contains various items such as depreciation and accruals which do not affect the bank overdraft at all – they are purely accounting entries. By charging up depreciation of £2,000 on the business equipment, the profit is reduced or the loss is increased but this does not affect the bank overdraft. Similarly, part of the year's loss may have been financed by the creditors – the creditors are owed more at the end of the year than at the beginning. This has not affected the bank overdraft at all. It will do so later when the creditors are paid, but not yet. The loss may also be related to a movement in the debtors and again this will not affect the bank overdraft. When it comes to the drawings, you may find that the Proprietor has drawn out a regular amount each week but he might also have had debited to his account various items which have not yet been paid – for example the tax liability of the business for the year. If the business made profits last year the tax will be payable this year and some provision for tax ought to be made – but at the balance sheet date it may not have been paid. If the Proprietor has been charged with it his drawings will be more than he actually drew – and the bank overdraft will not have been increased until the tax is paid.

Accounts, even quite simple accounts, contain many items of this nature and it is important that they are identified. The profit or loss goes up and down by virtue of many things, a number of which do not affect the bank balance at all and if the Inland Revenue are going to restrict your bank interest relief you must exclude these items from the calculation. Do not let yourself be bamboozled into agreeing an adjustment to your profits without all the proper calculations being made. Very often you will find that when the details are looked into, the problem disappears entirely but you will still need to persuade the Inspector of Taxes. I recall one case where the Inspector of Taxes was arguing this point and it was shown that throughout the period that the Proprietor had overdrawn his capital account, the bank account was actually in credit, but that did not stop him trying to disallow the overdraft interest for other periods.

Eventually he understood what he was arguing about but it took a long time. It is most unsatisfactory that Inspectors of Taxes put forward arguments which they do not understand and say things like 'I trust that you will now be able to agree and withdraw your claim' when they have no idea about what they are saying. However, we have to live in the real world and not how we would like it to be, and this is an area where some detailed explanation will be necessary for the taxman if you are going to stave off an increased tax charge.

I have dwelt at length on this rather complicated point mainly as an example that sometimes the Inland Revenue take a firm stance on a technical matter and try to browbeat you into agreeing with their apparently plausible view. Such views should be analysed carefully to see whether they stand up to proper scrutiny and if not they should always be firmly, and courteously, rejected.

## Overdrawn Directors' Loan Accounts

This sounds a somewhat obscure matter but is of widespread application to many small family companies – and larger companies. A long time ago the Inland Revenue realized that directors of companies could avoid large amounts of tax by not having any salary from the company but by simply having loans from the company instead. The loans were not taxable because they were not salaries, and although the loans were repayable, there were not in fact repaid for years (if at all,) and this was a means of supplying the directors with a great deal of tax free money.

However, the Inland Revenue wised up (they always do in the end) and if a director now borrows any money from his company it not only has legal consequences under the Companies Acts, it also has some serious tax disadvantages. Not only will the director pay tax on a benefit in kind by reason of having the benefit of such a loan (the taxable benefit will be a notional amount of interest he would have paid for having such a loan) but in addition the company will have to pay over to the Inland Revenue a sum equal to one third of the amount of the loan; however, this latter sum is repaid to the company by the Inland Revenue when the loan is repaid by the director. This is enough to discourage such loans but there is further problem of disclosure. You have to tell the Inland Revenue that such a loan has been made so that he can charge the appropriate tax. If you do not tell him, or perhaps more commonly you only give him a few clues so that he might deduce the position, you will end up with a hefty charge to interest on the unpaid tax and a penalty. It is not enough to put the loan to the director in debtors – that is what it is, a debtor of the company – it must be separately identified, either in the accounts, by note, or in the correspondence, so that the Inland Revenue know that the loan has been made and can assess the tax. If you do not show clearly that the loan has been made to the director, the Inland Revenue will be down on you like a ton of bricks – indeed they may well regard it as fraudulent and will not only charge interest and penalties but may take a more serious line.

The director will not escape either because he will also be liable to a tax on his benefit in kind and if this has not been disclosed there will be interest and penalties on him as well. This can prove to be a very expensive process indeed but it will not end there. This will be regarded by the Inland Revenue as sufficient to throw doubt on the accuracy of your company's accounts and an in-depth enquiry will probably ensue. Similarly, the directors, who are inevitably mixed up in all this, will also have their affairs investigated in depth and you will be on the wrong end of a very wide-ranging and expensive investigation.

If you are in the position of finding a director owing the company money at the end of the year (and after the end of the year is too late to do anything about it – don't even think of back-dating a document to put it right or you will add criminal liability to your other problems) it is well worth while making sure that the amount is repaid as soon as possible i.e. before the accounts are finalised so that a note can be made in the accounts to the effect that the amount has been repaid. In many cases this will discourage the Inland Revenue from taking the matter further and provided you do not do it too often no problems should arise. It is not difficult for the director to borrow money from his bank to repay the loan to the company – the payment into the company will of course go into the company's bank account so as far as the bank is concerned they are no worse off (providing of course the director and the company are with the same bankers); the director will even obtain tax relief for any interest paid on the borrowings so there is little reason not to rearrange the financing to put this right.

Whatever you do, you should not cover it up by repaying the amount just before the end of the year and drawing it out again early in the following year. This is not a matter that can be concealed, not least because the Companies Act requires loans to directors during the year to be separately identified, and failure to make this disclosure will give rise to serious implications when the Inland Revenue find out. You may be assured that penalty proceedings will follow.

Until recently it was common practice for the amount owing by the director at the end of the year to be effectively repaid by voting him a sufficient salary after the end of the year. This is no longer possible and anybody who tries to do this will incur the justifiable wrath of the Inland Revenue – not because the Inland Revenue say so but because this accounting treatment has been specifically stated by the professional accountancy bodies to be incorrect. The salary had not been voted to the director at the year end and should not therefore be credited to his account; it should be shown in creditors and not be deducted from the amount he owes to the company. The Inland Revenue know all about this (do not delude yourself into thinking that it is an obscure matter of accounting theory which they do not appreciate – they have been specifically instructed on the matter) and if your accounting treatment is wrong to this extent they will certainly point out that the accounts are not prepared in accordance with proper accounting principles. You can therefore expect to be investigated fully – after all if you prepare accounts incorrectly in this respect, they may well expect to find other irregularities by a searching enquiry.

One way of avoiding these problems is to arrange for the directors to have a Service Contract so that their salaries accrue to them evenly month by month and can therefore be credited to their loan accounts before the year end net of PAYE. Alternatively, the position can be corrected by paying a dividend to the shareholders before the year end; indeed this may be a better solution (as dividends are not liable to national insurance contributions) but what ever you do to remedy the situation at the year end, the action must be taken before that date.

## Ramsey and Furniss v. Dawson

These names are beloved by the taxman because they represent
a series of decisions in the courts whereby taxpayers have tried
to avoid tax by artificial means. These cases created what is
known as the 'new approach' to curbing the avoidance of tax
and they are trotted out as a sort of talisman or code word to
say that you should not be given a particular tax relief you are
claiming. Unless you are professionally advised you will very
rarely have anything to do with the principle enshrined by these
cases but occasionally the Inland Revenue do mention them and
you should be aware of what they mean – and more importantly
what they do not mean.

In both cases a series of transactions were undertaken by
the taxpayer and the courts decided, in very broad terms, that
if you have a series of transactions which looked at as a whole
should be properly regarded as a single composite transaction,
they can look at the beginning and the end, and ignore the
intermediate steps. A simple example would be for you to give
your wife an asset which she then sells to take advantage of
some relief or exemption so that no tax arises, whereupon she
gives the money back to you. This would probably fall down on
basic principles but if not the taxman could say that this was a
series of transactions and the intermediate step (i.e. the gift to
your wife) had no purpose other than the avoidance of tax and
they can therefore ignore the wife's involvement and treat the
disposal as being made by you so that the relief or exemption
you were seeking would not be available.

The principles involved are extremely complex and it is not
at all easy for the Inland Revenue to actually succeed with
such an argument when they get into the technical details.
The response to any suggestion by the Inland Revenue that
Furniss v. Dawson applies is simply to say that it does not –
and to say the magic words of your own which are 'Craven
v. White'. This recent case severely limits the extent of the
Furniss v. Dawson approach because unless all the steps in your
plan are actually predetermined, you should be safe. This shows
that there will usually be an appropriate defence to the Inland
Revenue taking this line and you should not be frightened or
bamboozled out of your defence by the Inland Revenue making
aggressive statements about the new approach or Furniss v.
Dawson.

## Tax Repayments

With the collection and administration of tax becoming more and more complicated the chances of errors in the Inland Revenue system going undetected must inevitably increase. Every day hundreds of people pay tax and hundreds of people receive repayments of tax they have overpaid and it is inevitable that sometimes a tax repayment will be made to somebody by mistake.

What should you do if you receive a tax repayment from the taxman knowing that it is wrong? This is a very important question because if you give the wrong answer you could find yourself in court. The Theft Act 1968 is wide enough to cover this situation and if you *know* that the taxman has made a mistake and has paid money to you as a result, you will be committing theft if you decide to keep the money and not tell the taxman. You may think this is a silly rule – if the Inland Revenue make a mistake it is not for you to correct them – why should you suffer serious consequences because of their mistake? Unfortunately, whether the rule is silly or not, it does exist as a number of people have found out to their cost. By way of example there is a recent case concerning a woman police officer who was by mistake paid overtime of £74 for a day when she was not working. The court decided that in these circumstances a dishonest intention to keep the money and not return it to the employers once the error had been discovered was undoubtedly theft. The application of this principle to a tax repayment is obvious and if you decide to keep quiet and hold on to the money knowing that you are not entitled to it, you run a serious risk of being charged with theft when the Inland Revenue find out.

Whilst this can be stated in simple terms, real life is a little more complicated and criminal charges require proof. Unless you are extremely knowledgeable about tax matters and assiduous in checking everything you receive from the Inland Revenue, it may be very difficult to have any certainty that a tax repayment you may receive is right or wrong. It would not be unreasonable to assume that as the Inland Revenue do not make repayments without a good deal of verification (some would say that it is like getting blood out of a stone), the amount you have received is probably right. You may not understand why the repayment has been sent to you but that does not mean it is wrong. By keeping it you are not acting dishonestly in any way. If, however, you do carefully check the amount received (you may want to check the repayment is not too little) and find that it is wrong for example because of a simple arithmetical error in your favour, you ought at the very least to tell the Inland Revenue, thereby indicating that you have no intention of permanently depriving them of their money.

An important point to note here is that this only applies where you actually receive some money. If you have merely been undercharged for tax you are under no duty to tell the Inland Revenue nor to correct the position for them. You may run the risk of being charged to interest on the amount underpaid in certain circumstances, when they ultimately find out their mistake, and for this reason you may feel like telling the Inland Revenue so that interest does not continue to run against you, but that is another matter.

You should, however, make sure that the reason why you have been undercharged is not because of any failure on your part to provide full and timely information. If the reason for the undercharge can be laid at your door, you will not only be liable to interest but you may be liable to a penalty as well. However, providing you are sure that all necessary information has been supplied and that the Inland Revenue have just made an error resulting in you paying less tax than you ought, then you are in the clear. They still have six years in which to correct the position but after that period has elapsed they can only pursue you for the undercharged tax if they can show neglect, wilful default or fraud on your part.

## Aiding and Abetting

One anxiety which many people express is whether they do wrong by paying somebody in cash. The scene will be familiar; you engage a man to do some work on your roof and he says it will cost say £2,000 providing you pay in cash. This has rather a sinister ring about it: perhaps he has something to hide. The most obvious conclusion is that he is not going to tell the Inland Revenue about the receipt of this money and he will not pay tax on it. By paying him in cash do you expose yourself to any penalty either under the Taxes Acts or under the criminal law?

Some people take a very firm view that you are not concerned at all with the other person and his tax affairs. You are not your brother's keeper. On a more technical level your relationship is based solely in contract. He has agreed to work for you – you have agreed the terms of payment with him and they do not involve any implication of wrongdoing. Coins of the Realm (and notes) are legal tender and it is quite proper for any number of reasons for him to insist on being paid in cash; if that is a term of the contract between you, you are obliged to pay him in cash. He may not have a bank account (whether you think it is desirable for him to have one is not at all relevant – you may think that it would be desirable for him to have a hair cut or use more deodorant but that is not relevant either); he may need the cash to pay his suppliers or he may not be happy to accept a cheque from you. It may be for any reason and it has nothing to do with you. The point behind all this is whether he is going to include the amount you pay him in his business accounts or otherwise disclose it to the Inland Revenue. You do not know, you are not entitled to know and if you ask him, he will probably respond in fairly robust terms. You may have suspicions about him and may feel that he is not the sort of person who deals properly with his tax affairs but it is not your business. However he deals with his private affairs is a matter between him and the Inland Revenue and you have no part of it. You could, if you wanted to be particularly unneighbourly, contact the Inland Revenue and the Customs & Excise and tell them that you have had work done on your roof and that you had paid Mr Bloggs £2,000 for doing it. They will always be pleased to receive this information because it will enable them to make a specific check that the relevant amounts are returned to his business accounts. However, this is a pretty unpleasant thing to do because it presupposes that the other person is dishonest – a supposition based purely on prejudice.

There is another view. The alternative view is that by agreeing to pay the worker in cash you are aiding and abetting the commission of a crime, the relevant crime here being the ancient common law offence of Cheating Her Majesty's Revenue. In the simplest case when you merely agree to pay in cash it is difficult to say that there is any or sufficient knowledge (or wilful blindness) on the part of the payer to represent the guilty mind which is an essential element of such a crime. There is no indication that any crime is going to be committed, merely an unfounded suspicion; furthermore you are not even putting him in a position to enable a crime to be committed because he could just as well fail to disclose the receipt to the Inland Revenue if you paid him by cheque. On these simple facts you do not have a problem – after all what are you going to say when your window cleaner asks you for his money for cleaning your windows? Are you going to pay him £10 only by cheque on condition that he gives you a formal invoice, sequentially numbered showing all the relevant details and a statement that part of your contractual arrangements are that he will be disclosing the receipt to the Inland Revenue? The very idea is absurd; even the Chairman of the Board of Inland Revenue has said that he pays his window cleaner in cash, there being no reason to think that the window cleaner does not pay his taxes like everybody else. In any event, he says, it is quite reasonable for window cleaners to want to be paid in cash.

However, the position may be more straightforward; the man coming to mend your roof for £2,000 may nod, wink, put his finger on his nose, or make some other sign or gesture which is intended to convey (and does convey) the clear message that the transaction will be concealed from the tax authorities. Indeed, it might even be put to you that if you want to pay by cheque, or if you want an invoice for the work done, it will cost 15% more. No offence would seem to be committed under the Taxes Act as a result of making such an agreement on this basis – but there would seem to be a much stronger case for suggesting that you are either aiding and abetting him to defraud the Inland Revenue or that you are conspiring with him to do so. In these circumstances each would know what was passing through the other's mind and the payment in cash would be the means of assisting the other party to fulfil his intended purpose. The possibility of conspiracy is more remote because conspiracy requires an agreement between the parties to carry out a course of action which would necessarily involve the commission of an offence. The offence involved here would be the dishonest concealment of the receipt from the Inland Revenue. You are not concerned with the other person's tax affairs and cannot influence him in any way so it is difficult to say that you could possibly have agreed that this would be a course of action to be carried out. However, there does remain the clear possibility of aiding and abetting.

So if you are faced with somebody whose contractual terms for carrying out the work are cash only and it is made plain that the price would be increased if the taxman or the VAT man knew about it you may justifiably feel a little nervous (so might he – he would not have been the first moonlighter to have suggested such terms to an Inspector of Taxes). It would be as well in these circumstances for you to obtain an invoice for the work done and a receipt for the payment.

You could explain that payment in cash would be inconvenient for you and that a cheque or banker's draft would be greatly preferred. If he gives you some sensible and *bona fide* reason for requiring payment in cash there would seem to be little difficulty in you agreeing to this as a term of the contract. You ought to do something, because it is long established that you can be liable as a aider and abetter even if you are indifferent to the point at issue – e.g. if a man deliberately sells to another a gun to be used for murdering a third person he is still guilty, even if he does not know who the victim is. Not knowing how the crime might be committed does not matter. An example here would be driving somebody armed with various weapons to a particular place knowing that he is going there specifically to kill somebody. You may not know the identity of the intended victim nor do you know how the offence is to be committed but this will still be enough to put you away.

These examples are rather dramatic and far removed from paying an odd job man in cash but the principles remain the same – crime is crime.

The position is not at all the same in connection with VAT where there exists an obscure provision which could make you liable to extremely severe penalties. The provision is not at all well known nor is it easy to understand but it says that if you are 'knowingly concerned in the fraudulent evasion of VAT' by somebody else or if you are 'knowingly concerned in the taking of steps with a view to the fraudulent evasion of VAT' by somebody else you could be liable to an unlimited fine and up to seven years in prison. This is pretty serious stuff and it is extremely wide in its application. However, it does require you to be *knowingly* concerned with the fraudulent evasion – having well founded suspicions would not be enough – but you only need to be concerned in the 'taking of steps with a view to' the other person's fraudulent evasion of VAT. The taking of steps could easily include the agreement to pay in cash after being told that the price is set because the taxman will not know about it, and again it only needs the steps to be taken 'with a view' to the evasion of VAT. If the roof man tells you that this is his intention, the steps are clearly taken with tax evasion in mind that that could lead you into the most serious difficulties.

Essentially the point here is that if the roof man is proposing fraudulently to evade tax and wants you to help him, you do so at your peril. It is very wise therefore to take a fairly vigorous stance when the subject of cash is being mentioned and to tell him that you will not help him in any way or countenance or condone any attempt by him fraudulently to evade VAT and explain the risks you will be taking by doing so. If he is wise he will keep his mouth tightly shut about his intentions but by definition he will not be very wise if he is attempting fraudulently to evade VAT in the first place. This may well mean that you will have to pay more for your roof repairs or that you will have to get the work done by somebody else, but that is greatly preferred to being sucked into a VAT investigation and the possibility of such serious consequences.

## *Extradition*

It is widely known that once you are outside the country and therefore beyond its jurisdiction the Inland Revenue have great difficulty in collecting any outstanding tax liabilities you leave behind – unless of course you have assets in the UK which the Inland Revenue can seize or obtain a charge over to satisfy any tax liability. The general rule is that the courts of one country will not directly or indirectly enforce the revenue laws of another and this is no doubt used by many people as a means of evading their proper liabilities to tax. The UK does not have any tax clearance procedure for people leaving the country, but this does not stop the Inland Revenue writing to taxpayers who are abroad asking them in fairly firm terms to pay their taxes and if necessary to take action for recovery through the courts. Whilst this may be thought of as a complete waste of time because even if the Revenue obtains judgement it cannot be enforced outside their jurisdiction, it is still very helpful for them to have an outstanding judgement in case the taxpayer returns to the UK.

The general rule against enforcement of the revenue laws of another country has the additional effect that you cannot be extradited for revenue offences to the UK. It has been fairly long established that even if the activities were themselves criminal, provided they have some connection with tax evasion, that was enough for the Inland Revenue to be prevented from enforcing their claim in the foreign court. However, in 1988 the position changed with the case which goes by the title of R v. Chief Metropolitan Stipendiary Magistrate *ex parte* Secretary of State for the Home Department (1988). What the court decided in this case was that the general rule against enforcement did not apply to criminal offences which are independent of revenue offences, even if they have a revenue connection. This would seem to be a most powerful weapon in the hands of the Inland Revenue because in many cases it may be possible to re-categorise a tax offence as a crime (see for example Chapter 7 dealing with the common law offence of Cheating Her Majesty's Revenue) which would be a good start. This is a complex area of law and a mere change in the wording of the offence is unlikely to be sufficient to bring the taxpayer screaming into the arms of the Inland Revenue. However, those who are planning to sit, champagne in hand, by the pool of their island paradise, supposedly safe from the clutches of the Inland Revenue, might do well to notice some dark clouds forming on the horizon.

*Chapter Nine*

# INTEREST AND PENALTIES

# INTEREST ON UNPAID (OR OVERPAID) TAX

If you do not pay your tax on time the taxman will make you pay interest on the unpaid tax. The rate of interest is high and it does not qualify for any tax relief so it is very expensive if you are able to claim tax relief for interest paid on your overdraft. The rate of interest varies in accordance with prevailing interest rates and at the time of writing it is 13 per cent so if you are wondering whether you should pay your tax on time you should bear this carefully in mind. If you are in business it will usually be cheaper to pay the tax by increasing your overdraft; the additional bank overdraft interest you will pay will be more than the interest that the taxman would charge, but you will get tax relief for the interest which will make it considerably cheaper.

The due date for paying tax depends upon the type of income and the type of tax but generally on business profits, income tax is payable in two equal instalments on 1 January and 1 July, capital gains tax is payable on 1 December following the year of assessment and corporation tax is payable nine months after the company's year end. If you have sent in your tax return on time, or at least by 31 October, you will probably receive an assessment before the due date of payment of the tax but if not the due date of payment will be thirty days after the assessment is issued.

It is possible to avoid interest for a little while by applying for 'postponement' – that is asking for some or all of the tax not to be payable on the due date because for some reason it is wrong. If you do this the tax will not be payable until the final amount is agreed – but watch out because interest on the postponed amount will still run after six months from the due date. So if you get your calculations wrong (or deliberately postpone too much) you will find yourself paying interest unexpectedly.

You can play a trick on the Inland Revenue by making a small claim for postponement (say £50) because until the Inspector of Taxes agrees the amount of the postponed tax, interest does not run on the rest of the tax payable until he does agree the postponed amount, or until six months has elapsed whichever happens first. This is not a procedure viewed favourably by the Inland Revenue and unless the figures are really large you will probably do yourself more harm than good by trying this more than once. The Inland Revenue will rumble you immediately and although they cannot do anything about it, they will make quite sure that you do not get the opportunity again by paying extremely careful attention to your tax affairs in future. It will be apparent from other chapters in this book that even if your tax affairs are in apple pie order it does not pay to have the Inland Revenue breathing down your neck. It can be irritating and expensive and if you slip up on some minor matter (e.g. miss a time limit) they will be merciless.

The above deals with the position with what might be called 'ordinary' interest, but there is also 'penalty' interest which arises when you have been neglectful. It is payable at the same rate but it invariably turns out to be more because of the dates from which it is charged. This is dealt with below under the heading of Neglect. (See page 127).

Another trap awaits you if you want to play ducks and drakes with your tax payments. If the assessment you receive is inadequate, you do not avoid interest on the amount undercharged by simply appealing against the assessment and paying the tax shown on the assessment. When in due course the taxman revises the assessment to put the figures right, interest will be charged from the date that it would have been charged if this extra amount had ben included in the original assessment, but you had postponed the tax. Accordingly you could be living in a fool's paradise by just paying up and keeping quiet. However, there is an exception. There is one circumstance when you can obtain an advantage and that is if you simply do not appeal against the inadequate assessment. If you are liable to pay (say) £10,000 in tax and the taxman has charged you only £5,000 you can simply let the assessment stand and wait for him to issue a new assessment to collect the balance. This will prevent him from charging interest on the extra amount until thirty days after the issue of the new assessment because he cannot 'revise' the old assessment — it would have become final and conclusive by your failure to appeal. But you must take care. If the assessment is inadequate because the taxman has not been provided with sufficient information to assess the right figure, you will find yourself considerably worse off because the taxman will regard this as the concealment of material information and will charge you penalty interest on the grounds of neglect and you will not only have failed to gain the advantage you seek – you will be positively disadvantaged. On the other hand if the Inspector of Taxes has been provided with all the necessary information but has just failed to assess the correct amount, you are free to use this tactic to avoid interest without any adverse consequences.

## Repayment Supplement

Before dealing with neglect it is necessary to look at the converse position – that is where the taxman owes you money because in that case he pays you interest; it is called repayment supplement. Just as interest on unpaid tax is very expensive so repayment supplement is extremely valuable. If you can earn a 13 per cent tax free return on your money elsewhere on your investments, this will not interest you very much, but for those who cannot do so, the Inland Revenue offer an excellent opportunity. Naturally however the rules for paying repayment supplement on overpaid tax are much stricter than the rules for paying interest on unpaid tax – but they can still be used to extremely good effect.

In general you do not get repayment supplement until one year after the end of the year of assessment to which the tax relates, or from 6 April following the date of the overpayment. So if you pay £10,000 tax on 1 October 1990 in respect of a liability for 1989/90 repayment supplement will not start running until 6 April 1991. If however you did not pay the tax until 30 April 1991, you would have to wait until 6 April 1992 before entitlement to supplement would start to run. (The due dates for the payment of corporation tax are different again but they follow the same general principle.) You therefore need to time your tax payments very carefully.

Whenever you receive an assessment it is well worth while considering the implications for repayment supplement because if you receive an assessment for the previous year in the early part of the next calendar year you may well want to make a substantial payment before 5 April so that supplement can be running while your tax is being agreed. If the assessment is wrong and wildly excessive do not worry – you can use it to your advantage. Let us assume that you receive an assessment for 1989/90 on 28 February 1991 and it shows tax chargeable of £20,000. You calculate that your tax liability is only going to be £5,000. If you pay the whole £20,000 on 31 March you will incur no interest because you will have paid the tax within thirty days from the date of the assessment and the excess £15,000 will be earning supplement at 13 per cent from 6 April. If the tax is not repaid until (say) 31 October you will receive over £1,000 supplement tax free. Indeed, you could do better than this and pay £30,000 so that £25,000 would be earning repayment supplement – it does not really matter how much you pay, you are going to receive interest at the same rate, although the larger the amount the more likely it is that the Inland Revenue will repay the excess quickly. Providing you get your dates right you are on to a winner. Furthermore, this also protects you from an unexpected interest charge in the event that your calculations are wrong and the tax turns out to be more than you expected.

Some people do not like paying more tax than they need on the grounds that it weakens their position if they are arguing that the tax is excessive. This should not be a real fear for two reasons. The first is that you can write to the Collector of Taxes explaining the position and expressing the payment to be 'without prejudice' so that it cannot be used against you; the second is that the Inspector of Taxes with whom you will be negotiating over the assessment will not know what tax you have paid because the communication between the Inspector and the Collector is extremely poor – in any event the Inspector is not concerned with payments of tax at all. You do need to take care with your dates because if you miscalculate the date you will not lose repayment supplement for only a short period, you will lose it for a whole year so it pays to make sure your figures are right. If you pay your tax very close to 5 April it is obviously important that you have evidence that the payment was made before and not after 5 April; if you are in danger of being too late with your payment you can always get your payment date-stamped by the Inland Revenue by paying it to the local Collector's office.

Obtaining repayment supplement in this way can be deeply satisfying and it is a technique which can also be used to good effect in connection with inheritance tax; this is explained in detail in Chapter 15.

## Neglect

This is a most important term in connection with taxation
because it is the key to whether the Inland Revenue will be
able to charge you interest and penalties on top of your tax
liability. It is a very wide term and means that you have failed
to do something that you ought to have done within the time
limit specified by the Taxes Acts. It is extremely difficult always
to comply with every single obligation under the Taxes Acts and
you may need some arguments to wriggle out of a charge of
neglect. The first possibility is the statutory defence which is
that 'a person shall be deemed not to have failed to do anything
required to be done within a limited time if he did it within
such further time, if any, as the Board or the Commissioner
or officer concerned may have allowed; and where a person had
a reasonable excuse for not doing anything required to be done
he shall be deemed not to have failed to do it unless the excuse
ceased, and after the excuse ceased, he shall be deemed not to
have failed to do it if he did it without unreasonable delay after
the excuse had ceased.'

This is an extremely useful provision and you should not fail
to bring it to the attention of the taxman if he accuses you of
being neglectful. You should note that you will be deemed not
to have failed to do something if you did it within such further
time as the officer may have allowed. This obviously deals with
a situation where you have been specifically allowed further time
to do something, but there is no reason why it should not also
apply where you have been allowed further time by implication.
For example if you have been in the habit of sending in your
accounts one year late and no comment has ever been made,
it is at least arguable that because you have regularly been
allowed further time you should not be regarded as neglectful
until such time as the Inspector of Taxes says that he will
no longer allow you to be so late with your accounts. This
argument is given considerable added force by the CCSU case
which is explained in Chapter 2. Further, and even better, if you
have always conducted your affairs on a certain basis, perhaps in
common with many others in similar circumstances, the Inland
Revenue will be in some difficulty with the Taxpayers' Charter if
they penalise you and not everybody else. This will be a complete
denial of their express policy to treat all taxpayers the same if

they have similar circumstances. The opportunities for arguing that you have been given further time by implication are almost limitless and you should always argue along these lines if you are accused of neglect. The taxman will not always agree but if you do not argue you will be charged interest and penalties for neglect anyway. It is well worth having some arguments up your sleeve because even if they are only partly successful, they can save you a good deal of money.

*Interest*

If you really have been neglectful, you expose yourself to penalties and to penalty interest, which is sometimes known as section 88 interest. Section 88 interest is nasty because although it is charged at the same rate as ordinary interest it is charged from the date when the tax should originally have been paid. If therefore you are two or three years in arrears with your tax return, the section 88 interest could be substantial. You can avoid section 88 interest either by showing that you have not been neglectful or by concession under section 88 (4), but it is not worth wasting your time with section 88 (4). It does admittedly say 'the Board may at their discretion mitigate any interest due under this section' but this discretion is very rarely exercised. When it say 'the Board,' it does not mean the Inspector of Taxes, it means the Inland Revenue's Head Office so you have an uphill struggle. If section 88 applies you are usually better off negotiating a reduction in the penalty than trying to get the interest mitigated. However, there is one exception where you should argue vigorously for a reduction in the interest charge. You can argue that you should not be charged section 88 interest from day one because although you sent in your tax return or other information late, the Inland Revenue have themselves delayed matters and you are being charged interest for a period representing their own delay. On these grounds it is possible to persuade the taxman to charge interest only for the part of the period representing your delay and once they have agreed to this you are on much firmer ground when it comes to the negotiation on penalties.

Do not take any notice if they say that you should pay the interest for the entire period because the interest merely represents 'commercial restitution' for the Revenue not having had their tax. This is nonsense – there is nothing commercial about it at all. They do not charge you interest because of any principle of commercial restitution; they charge you interest because the Taxes Act says so and for no other reason. They soon deny the existence of any principle of commercial restitution when it comes to making tax repayments.

## Penalties

When it comes to penalties there is much more scope for flexibility because the penalties for neglect can go up to 100 per cent of the tax charged plus a fixed amount which varies according to the particular default – it is usually £300. These are the maximum penalties and are intended (like all maximum penalties) to be for the worst type of case. The penalties are always reduced from their maximum – in fact they are always reduced so much that the maximum figures become entirely irrelevant. So do not be alarmed if you get a letter from the taxman stating the maximum penalties; the Inspector is not serious and if he is you have good reason to complain. The taxman publishes various guidelines for penalty mitigation in connection with investigation cases but these are not adhered to with any consistency either and the matter is purely one of negotiation. You must dredge up every conceivable reason why you should not be regarded as neglectful (do not forget the reasonable excuse defence mentioned above) and always argue that even if you have been technically neglectful, a nominal penalty is all that is appropriate. This will take time but the time will be well spent.

After a period of negotiation you should consider carefully whether it will be worthwhile sending the Inspector of Taxes a cheque for the amount you are suggesting you should pay. With a cheque in his hand for a reasonable amount and the opportunity to close his file, human nature dictates that he will want to keep it rather than send it back and try to extract an extra amount. The Inland Revenue are not psychologically suited to sending money back to the taxpayer. However, you should not try this ploy too early, before a conclusion is actually on the horizon. It would simply be regarded as your first offer and probably drive up the amount of the eventual penalty rather than reduce it.

There is a provision relating to penalties which looks like a defence for the taxpayer (similar to that mentioned above for interest) but the taxman sometimes interprets it in a strange manner. It is section 97 Taxes Management Act 1970 and it says that if you send the taxman information or accounts and it later comes to your notice that they are wrong, you will be treated as being negligent unless you remedy the error without unreasonable delay.

This sounds helpful but some Inspectors of Taxes say that this provision is not a defence at all, merely an additional power for the Inland Revenue to claim a penalty. This can lead to arguments and it is helpful to know that the official Inland Revenue view revealed in a recent interview is that S97 does provide a defence of innocent error. This is a handy admission to have up your sleeve in case of difficulty (see Certified Accountant: October 1989 p.33).

It has been said by the Inland Revenue Head Office that only a small number of cases lead to a charge to penalties and this should never happen without the Inspector of Taxes following a formal procedure. Accordingly if at the outset of his enquiries the taxman says that any adjustment which might prove necessary as a result of his enquiries will also carry interest and penalties, he is almost certainly departing from his instructions. It may not seem to matter very much whether he is going to charge interest and penalties later – what matters is whether he actually does so. However, it is no bad thing to know that he is acting outside the proper procedures; the Inland Revenue do like their Inspectors to follow their instructions and it can do your case no harm at all to make it known (ever so gently) that you know .... He is not going to want to expose himself to criticism from his superiors and every little helps.

The key to successful penalty and interest negotiation is the same as in any other area of negotiation and that is to maintain your stance that you are being unfairly treated, that you are being forced into submission by pressure of time (and costs perhaps) and distraction from your business which you cannot afford – and everything else you can think of to support your case. Remember that the Inspector will not entirely agree – that is expecting too much, but if you bring all these factors into play you will almost certainly come to a favourable settlement in the end.

*Chapter Ten*

# REOPENING EARLIER YEARS

# REOPENING EARLIER YEARS

Sometimes the taxman, having looked into various aspects of your accounts for one year, decides that he would like to look again at the previous year's accounts. He will have only one purpose in mind; that is to charge you more tax for last year and probably earlier years as well. This is extremely serious because it will mean a lot of extra tax.

You may be rather anxious about this and wonder whether he really can go back to earlier years just like that. The taxman will explain that his reasons for doing so are that he has made a 'discovery'; he will point you to section 29(3) Taxes Management Act 1970 which says that if the Inspector discovers that any assessment to tax is insufficient, he may make an assessment for the amount which in his opinion ought to be charged. This is very impressive authority and becomes even more so when he tells you that 'discovery' means nothing more than the Inspector coming to an honest belief that there has been an under-assessment or even just changing his mind without any new facts coming to his attention.

In the face of such an explanation, anybody could be forgiven for concluding that, however unfair it seems, the taxman does have the power he claims to reopen earlier years and that there is nothing you can do about it.

Fortunately, there are some serious obstacles in the path of the taxman (unless of course he can find some default in the previous year) and it is no credit to the Inland Revenue that Inspectors pursue this line without necessarily having any entitlement to do so, nor giving the taxpayer any indication that they might be exceeding their powers.

In 1985 a very significant case was decided called Scorer v. Olin Energy Systems Ltd in which the ability of the taxman to reopen earlier years was examined at length. There being no higher legal authority than a decision of the House of Lords the Inland Revenue should not be permitted to disregard it.

The essential principle is that once an assessment has been issued and that your appeal against the assessment has been settled by agreement, that ought to be the end of the matter. You should not have to suffer the anxiety of wondering whether many years later the taxman is going to change his mind and charge you some more tax. For this principle to operate there must have been an assessment to tax and there must have been an appeal against it; the appeal may have been determined by a hearing by the Commissioners or, as is usually the case, will have been settled by agreement in writing with the taxman. Unless these three elements are present – assessment, appeal, and agreement – you have little protection. For this reason it is the practice in many accountants' offices to appeal against every assessment in principle (even if the figures are known to be right) just so that a determination by agreement can be obtained.

In these circumstances the power of the taxman to reopen earlier years and to issue further assessments for those years is strictly limited. To do so he must show that the point under consideration, that is the reason why he now wishes to charge you more tax, was not agreed at the time. The test of whether an agreement existed is whether, having regard to all the circumstances and the information available to the Inland Revenue, a reasonable man would have concluded that the Inspector had agreed the point. It is not necessary for the specific point to have been the subject of discussion or correspondence at the time; all that is required is for all the information necessary for an ordinarily competent inspector to have properly considered the matter should be in his possession. He may have made a mistake or misunderstood the facts before him or indeed failed to think about it at all; it does not matter. If you gave him all the relevant information and he agreed the liability for the earlier year, he cannot later change his mind (or make any other 'discovery' within the meaning of section 29(3) TMA1970) to issue a further assessment or charge more tax.

This is a very powerful protection but you must remember that it is only available where the information you provided to the taxman was complete and accurate; any shortcomings in the details provided or any ill-advised fudging of issues in your accounts could well be fatal to your argument.

*Chapter Eleven*

# INTERVIEWS WITH
# THE TAXMAN

# INTERVIEWS

One of the taxman's favourite ploys is to ask you to go to his office for an interview. In terms of your tax affairs, this is potentially the single most dangerous thing you can do.

It is conceivable (just about) that an interview will not give rise to any problems; you could have a really pleasant meeting with a kind and warm Inspector of Taxes who merely wants to clarify a few points so that he can settle your tax position quickly and easily. This is possible – but so is winning the pools. It might not be quite like that. You could have a most gruelling two or three hours with a really aggressive Inspector who gives you the third degree and you come away from it not only on the edge of a nervous breakdown but possibly with a huge tax liability which may not necessarily be justified.

The first thing to be aware of is that, however aggressive and demanding the Inspector of Taxes may be, he has no power to force you to attend an interview at his office. However, if you do refuse to go he will invariably take action because he will feel he is being frustrated; furthermore it would be very easy indeed for him to suggest that your refusal to attend an interview is deliberate non-cooperation with all sorts of sinister implications, and it may well be similarly viewed by the Commissioners if you eventually have to appear before them. Requests for interviews therefore have to be handled with great care.

You must consider the reason why the Inspector of Taxes has asked you for an interview. The chances are that he is on a thinly disguised fishing expedition. It needs to be disguised because fishing is a procedure not in keeping with the Inland Revenue guidelines on this subject, but of course it happens all the time. You should always bear in mind that there are no questions which the Inspector of Taxes can ask you at an interview that he cannot put to you in writing. He will say that it will be easier to resolve matters at an interview (easier for whom?) but this is just an excuse. He wants to question you closely on a wide range of subjects to see if anything pops up which leads him to charge some more tax – not only on you but possibly on other people as well.

Superficially this can hardly be criticized. If you are liable for some tax but because you have innocently failed to provide information to the Inland Revenue, the taxman is not able to charge you the right tax, and it is only right and proper that it should come out into the open so that you do not escape tax by inadvertence. However this superficial approach does not address the need for fairness and justice in the administration of the tax system.

By meeting the Inspector of Taxes face to face you are in a position of supreme disadvantage, not dissimilar to being in a boxing ring with Mike Tyson. It will not be a meeting of equals. The taxman has the knowledge and the technique and for all practical purposes you will be defenceless. The result will never be in doubt and you will not know what hit you – or even see it coming.

He will ask you lots of innocent sounding questions; some of them will be genuinely innocent and intended only to increase his understanding of your affairs, but others will be designed to provide him with an argument to charge tax.

There will be an initial period of general conversation during which he will probably try and find out what car you drive, what car your wife drives (and who pays for it), what sort of mileage you do on business, where you go on holiday, where your children are educated, what hobbies you have (anything really expensive like flying or motor racing) – and other domestic information. He is not being friendly; he is very seriously at work. He is trying to discover whether your living expenses are consistent with your income. If you spend £10,000 a year on holidays, another £10,000 on school fees and another £10,000 on various hobbies, all out of an income of £40,000 (which would leave you with about £30,000 a year after tax) he will wonder what your wife uses for money at the local supermarket. This will be the start of an in-depth investigation and is just the kind of result that he was hoping for with his fishing expedition.

The taxman can be extremely subtle with his enquiries and in the manner of his approach and you should therefore always be on your guard. I have heard Inspectors of Taxes ask the most outrageous question which to the well informed are obviously a deliberate trap, simply by using colloquial language to disguise what is in fact a highly technical question. This is simply not fair. What it does is to put the taxpayer at a considerable disadvantage so that if there is the slightest error it can be made to look much worse,and if there is nothing wrong at all it can be made to look as if there probably is. In most cases, the whole point of an interview is to enable the Inspector of Taxes to exploit the subtleties of the language of tax in his questions, and to prevent the taxpayer having any opportunity for proper consideration of his replies. It is intended to get him to make 'admissions' which give rise to a tax liability. The 'admissions' may in fact be entirely wrong statements based on a misunderstanding, but once they are made it is an uphill struggle to put the record straight.

## The Request

The request for an interview will always be made in writing by the Inspector of Taxes and he will sometimes, but not always, give you a reason. The first response must be to ask him why he feels the meeting is necessary, to which you will receive an airy fairy response that it will help him resolve outstanding issues. You should then ask him what those issues are. Again you will get a very general statement which on careful reading will be no answer at all. You should probe further and inquire what information he requires because you will be pleased to send it to him. This is important because at all times you should show yourself to be willing and able to attend an interview if it should serve any useful purpose, but that a general chat would be a waste of your time which you may not be able to spare from your business or your job. Once he has asked for an interview he is unlikely to withdraw the request for fear of losing face, so you will probably have to go along in the end. You need to prepare the ground well in advance so that when you actually meet the potential danger is minimised.

You should ask him for an agenda of the things he wants to discuss and the questions he wants to ask you. You will very rarely get either but the way in which he avoids giving you these details will indicate whether or not he is on a fishing expedition and you could make some oblique reference to the fact. Indeed you could draw attention to the Inland Revenue guidelines which say that where the taxpayer is professionally represented, the accountant should be given the chance to satisfy the Inspector before any meeting with the client is arranged. You can go further and stand firm, saying that you have answered all his questions fully and honestly and have provided him with all the information he has asked for and that if he wants anything further he should tell you. If he will not tell you, you will be unable to be very helpful at any interview because you will not go prepared with any of the information he may require. This will certainly flush him out because he will respond by saying that the questions he has in mind will not need any research or preparation – and he has therefore opened the door wide for you to ask what questions he does have in mind. It is now his turn to be on the defensive and you should do nothing to lessen his unease. You can at this point agree to a meeting if he provides details of what he wants to ask and discuss. You will eventually get something from him and you can start your probing some more but do not go too far or it will look like prevarication and you will lose the initiative.

## The Interview

The time that the meeting takes place can be highly relevant to its outcome. This may sound absurd, but the Inspectors of Taxes are not self-employed and therefore like to stick fairly closely to their normal working hours. If you therefore arrange the meeting for 3.30p.m. or preferably 4.00p.m. you may well find that as 5.00p.m. approaches the Inspector will be less disposed to broaden the scope of his questions unless there is a real point to them. This will concentrate his mind on to the questions of the most relevance, because he will want to be going home. This is particularly true on Fridays. If the meeting is to take place in the morning, 11.00a.m. or 11.30a.m. is a good time to start because as the time gets towards 12.30p.m. he will be thinking about having some lunch. This really is an excellent way to shorten the meeting because you can be quite sure that if the meeting starts at 9.30a.m. it will still go on until lunchtime because he will have set the morning aside for the interview. The time at which the meeting takes place ought to be your decision, not his, and you should be firm about arranging it at your convenience, bearing the above in mind. But do not overdo it. If you suggest 8.30a.m. or 5.00p.m. he will rumble you. He really cannot suggest that 11.00a.m. or 3.30p.m. is an unreasonable hour and this ought to give him enough (but not too much) time to ask all his questions. If he wants more time you can always come back another day (but you can be appropriately indignant later about having to attend two interviews); if he suggests it will take longer than one and a half hours or so, you have an additional reason to ask him why the matters involved should take so long; they really must be pretty serious and you would want to have a lot more details.

It is highly likely that despite all your efforts when the interview eventually takes place you will have very little more than a list of a few general areas which he intends to cover. You should make quite sure that he does not go outside them, and if he does stray beyond the specified areas you can ask him why – there ought to be a good reason for him to do so; particularly if he asks a lot of personal and sometimes extremely intimate questions about your private life.

At the interview you would be well advised, after the initial preliminaries, to take the bull by the horns and start the interview yourself. He has got you there to ask you questions about x – what is it that he would like to know and what has it got to do with your tax liability? You will eventually lose the initiative because he will have prepared very carefully for the meeting and for the questions he is going to ask (something you will not be able to do). Do not be alarmed. If you do not know the answer to a question say so. Never, never guess and never volunteer possibilities. The best response is to say that you do not know or you cannot remember and you will find out the answer and let him know. If he presses the point you can quite reasonably say that it would be wrong for you to give him an answer that you cannot be sure of and you will give him the information as soon as you have looked into it. You may have to say this a number of times. Whatever you do, never try to give him the response you think sounds good or is somehow to your advantage. You have no idea what will be advantageous and what will not and if you do this you are doomed. Stick rigidly to the facts and to the truth – if you do not, you will be even more doomed. I remember one occasion visiting an Inspector of Taxes when the question was asked whether the client drank or smoked. The client, realizing that this question was aimed at assessing his usual expenditure, denied that he did either. Unfortunately the papers which he had given to the Inspector of Taxes reeked of cigar smoke. Whatever he was trying to achieve by departing from the truth, he certainly failed, and an immediate (and prompted) admission that he did not smoke *cigarettes* repaired only some of the damage.

Do not allow the Inspector to put words into your mouth. You can bet that any words he does put into your mouth will not be to your advantage so beware. Remember all those TV interviews with politicians who are asked all kinds of nasty questions by reporters. However hard the interviewer tries, they explain the position in their own words and if pressed they explain it all again in their own words. If they did not do so, they would assuredly be trapped by skilful cross examination – and so would you be, and very much more easily.

The possibility has to be acknowledged that the Inspector of Taxes may be able to show that you are somehow in default with your tax liabilities and he will explain the nature of your default. This is unfortunate and clearly puts you at a disadvantage. All you can do is express surprise or sorrow and to promise to investigate the reasons for it. Do not be led into answering the question 'why did you . . . ' or 'why did you not . . . ', but say that you will let him know. You must be firm at this point or you will live to regret your ill-considered statements. However, there is one circumstance where you should make some response and that is when a denial would reasonably be expected – as a sort of gut reaction. If you did something or did not do something because you simply did not know that is a quite reasonable response; but do not elaborate. You will only make matters worse – you will have been taken by surprise and that is not a good position from which to start making explanations. Wait until you get home, think about it carefully and put forward the explanation in writing.

Always remember that the Inspector of Taxes is making notes of everything you say – there are no asides or off-the-record comments in an interview with the taxman. It all goes down and if it can be used against you, it will. For this reason you should, preferably at the beginning, ask the Inspector of Taxes if he will supply you with a copy of his notes of the meeting. He will nearly always agree to do so. However, if he does not, ask him again and note down verbatim his response. The Inland Revenue have publicly stated that they see no grounds for the Inspector doing other than meeting the request to supply copies of notes. But keep this up your sleeve. If he is the type of Inspector that would refuse you a copy of his notes he is going to make other errors of judgement too and you had better write them all down; when you resume the correspondence after the meeting you will have a much longer list of justified grievances. In any event you should always take your own notes and if he says anything you think is important – either technical or informal (particularly if it is obviously to your disadvantage) be very careful to note down exactly what he says. Do not be harried into not doing so – if he carries on with his questions, ask him to wait until you have completed your notes.

It really puts the taxman off if you keep writing down his exact words because he knows that he therefore has to take extra care – and he will not be used to that in interviews with taxpayers. Fortunately, notes taken by Inspectors of Taxes are generally of a very high standard and when you receive your copy you will probably be surprised at their comprehensiveness and their accuracy. You should always of course compare them with your own notes and immediately point out any differences, just so that his version of the meeting is not accepted by default. Take particular care over nuances of language which might give rise to a misleading impression. All these should be corrected in writing without undue delay.

There is one situation in which you should immediately be on your guard and that is if there are two taxmen in the room when you arrive. You should find out who the second person is and ask why he is there. He will either be more senior than the Inspector you have been dealing with, or more junior. If he is more senior you deserve an explanation because it may mean that the matter is far more serious than you have been led to believe. If so you should apologise and say that you need to postpone the meeting until you have taken professional advice. He will not like this but it is irresistible and you must, must, must stand firm. If you do not, and allow the interview to proceed, you will cause untold damage to your position.

If the other person is a junior colleague the position is not much better but you have no real excuse to leave. The problem is that in the presence of a junior colleague the Inspector will want to show off – to demonstrate how he can get the better of the taxpayer. He cannot afford to display any generosity or any flexibility of approach in case his junior thinks he is being weak; furthermore he can never let you get the better of him in any argument. You are in deep trouble here and you are on your own. This is one of the main reasons why it is best never to attend an interview with the taxman without a professional adviser. You can still be taken by surprise but at least your professional adviser would even up the odds because the Inspector of Taxes will be under scrutiny from both sides.

## Professional Assistance

It will be apparent from the above that you venture alone into the lion's den at your peril. A competent professional adviser will be of enormous help at any interview because he at least will know the ropes: he will be able to see traps before they are sprung and clarify all areas of misunderstanding to your advantage. The point is perhaps too obvious to warrant explanation – he will protect you. However, he does need to be competent. An incompetent professional adviser will do you more harm than good because if you are steam-rollered by the Inspector of Taxes he will later be able to say that you were professionally represented and that if there was anything untoward going on your representative should have said something at the time.

Any competent professional adviser will have taken you through all the points the Inspector might raise in advance and given you a full briefing; he will also give you a taste of how tough the questions might be so that you are not taken by surprise. But do not expect him to do all the talking at the interview. He will be able to interrupt to clarify various points or to prevent you being harassed into saying unwise things, but if he overdoes his protection and does not let you answer the questions freely and fully, he will give the impression that you have something to hide. You must always answer the questions yourself, honestly and preferably without his help; the less the adviser has to do at the meeting the better. If at every question you look to him to give you the right answer, the taxman will not unnaturally become extremely suspicious. But if you answer the question in your own words from your own knowledge, pausing only long enough to allow your adviser to add any comment by way of clarification which may be necessary, you will give a far better impression and the Inspector of Taxes will be much more ready to accept what you say.

There is one circumstance where an interview with the Inspector of Taxes is of really positive value to you and that is where the Inspector thinks you have been concealing information or acting dishonestly. You will rarely if ever dispel such an impression by correspondence. You have to go and see him and show him by your answers to his questions and by your general demeanour that you are an honest person and that whatever may have gone wrong (if anything) it would not have been by

deception or deliberate wrong-doing but by accident. This will do
you a power of good because otherwise the Inspector's suspicions
will simply fester and you will end up with a large assessment to
tax based only on his suspicions. However, in such circumstances
you should never be without your professional adviser because
if something *has* gone wrong you need him to show the Inspector
of Taxes that you are serious about putting everything right and
that this is the man who is going to do it.

In conclusion you should always bear in mind the following
golden rules when it comes to interviews:

1) Clarify the issues from the outset.
2) Do not talk too much.
3) Stick rigidly to the truth.

And above all get professional advice.

*Chapter Twelve*

# THE KEITH COMMITTEE

# THE KEITH COMMITTEE

You do not have to be involved in correspondence very long with the taxman before he starts mentioning the Keith Committee – particularly if there is any element of neglect involved. It is important to know what this is all about because otherwise it is just a magic word – one which will put you at a disadvantage. You would be unlikely to know what the Keith Committee is, let alone what it said and have no way of sensibly countering such an approach by the Inland Revenue. Accordingly a few words of explanation about the Keith Committee may be helpful.

The Keith Committee was set up in 1980 for the specific purpose of enquiring into and reporting on the tax enforcement provisions of the Inland Revenue and the Customs and Excise, to consider whether their existing powers were suitable for ensuring compliance with the law, and in particular to avoid excessive burdens on tax payers. The committee did a thorough job and made a large number of recommendations about how to improve the tax administration. The report goes into three volumes over one thousand pages and although it is essential reading for those advising professionally on tax matters, it is unbelievingly boring to anybody else and at £35 is rather expensive as a source of background information.

The report was examined closely by all concerned, i.e. accountants, lawyers and the Inland Revenue, and the general conclusion was that, taken as a whole, it represented a balanced package of recommendations for improving the enforcement of taxes. Unfortunately, and to their great discredit, the Inland Revenue have managed to destroy all balance and fairness inherent in the recommendations. They have quite simply rejected those which they did not agree with (it would be nice if we as taxpayers could have rejected those with which we did not agree). Other recommendations have been deferred and others have been implemented, but with modifications. In fact the selective and piecemeal implementation is highly prejudicial to the taxpayer. It is for this reason that you should not be over-impressed when an Inspector of Taxes refers to the Keith Committee as some kind of endorsement for his approach.

However, despite these rather serious disadvantages, the Keith Committee did make a report and changes have been made to our tax enforcement rules. We have to make the best of the

rules which now exist. Fortunately, the Keith Committee report
does contain a great deal of information about Inland Revenue
procedures and departmental instructions which are simply not
available elsewhere, and in a form with which the Inland Revenue cannot readily disagree. They gave voluminous evidence
to the committee about Inland Revenue practice in many areas.
It is therefore not always as boring as it might appear and the
following miscellaneous points drawn from the report may be
of considerable help in negotiations with the Inland Revenue
when they suggest that you have dome something wrong, or
have failed to do something that you should have done.

A) 'A mistake is not a default provided it is drawn to the
Inland Revenue's attention as soon as the taxpayer becomes
aware of it.' (Paragraph 3. 5. 1.)
   This can be extremely helpful because it is not a view shared by
many Inspectors of Taxes. You can gain a great deal of initiative
by innocently putting forward this view, waiting for the Inspector
to say that you are quite wrong, and then giving him the Keith
Committee reference. It is, however, much more helpful to wait
until you have a number of such statements which effectively
make up the whole of the taxman's case against you. If you
can manoeuvre him into making such statements and then in a
simple letter dismantle the whole of his arguments by selected
references from the Committee's report, he will probably sink
without trace or die of embarrassment – or probably both.

B) An in-depth investigation is exactly what it says – it is
an investigation by the Inland Revenue into part of your tax
affairs (probably all of them) in great depth. If you have been
selected for an in-depth investigation you can consider yourself
unlucky because fewer than 3 per cent of cases are chosen for
this treatment. The Inland Revenue 'are not authorised to select
cases at random' (Paragraph 10. 2. 1) and it is unlikely that you
will be able to manoeuvre the Inspector of Taxes into saying that
you have been selected at random – this criticism is too well
known. However, providing that you have taken care with your
tax return and done absolutely nothing to indicate that there is
anything wrong with your return you should not be investigated
in depth.
   The main reasons for an investigation are either an unusual
gross profit percentage, unsatisfactory features about personal

expenditure such as under-adjustments for own consumption of stock, or where the Inland Revenue have information from a different source which does not match that shown in your return or your accounts. Other reasons could be various matters such as apparently high expenses, unexplained increases in wealth, and accounts being prepared by an unreliable person.

As suggested above, all these items should be looked into very carefully before submitting your tax return or any supporting accounts so that the chances of an expensive investigation are minimized. Furthermore, it gives great weight to your request for the disclosure of grounds if none of these matters can be regarded as unsatisfactory. You should always remember that the taxman may be working on inaccurate information supplied by a third party. You should not be put to a great deal of trouble and expense simply because somebody else has given him wrong information.

C) The Inland Revenue staff are 'instructed to be specific about the grounds for an in-depth investigation'. (Paragraph 10. 3. 1.) This again is an extremely helpful statement because Inspectors of Taxes are invariably reluctant about disclosing their grounds. However, this only holds good for in-depth investigations and does not apply to other enquiries such as those concerning possible omissions from a tax return where it is accepted Inland Revenue practice not to be specific. If therefore your affairs have been chosen for an in-depth investigation it is well worth asking why you have been put to the trouble and expense involved. This will deter the Inspector of Taxes from a general 'fishing expedition' which is a practice frequently complained of by the accountancy bodies and always denied by the Inland Revenue. If the Inspector of Taxes refuses to be specific about the reason why your case has been selected, do not fire off an immediate response of 'what about paragraph 10. 3. 1. of the Keith Committee report' – wait and see whether there will be a better opportunity for this shot later.

D) As noted above there is a requirement to notify the Inland Revenue of the existence of a new source of income, e.g. the commencement of a new business, and it is most helpful to find in the report a reference to an Inland Revenue practice whereby 'they regard an informal call to the tax office for explanations from a taxpayer setting up in business and

seeking help about complying with his tax affairs is sufficient to
satisfy the requirement to notify chargeability'. This again is not
a matter well known within the Inspectorate but you do have to
make sure that you keep an accurate record of such an informal
call. It is all too easy for a defaulting taxpayer to say that he did
make such a call and the Inland Revenue will naturally be very
sceptical; the Inspector of Taxes may have made no record on
his file or he may have moved to another tax district and they
may not accept that you actually made such a call. However, if
you have a contemporaneous written record (particularly with
the name of the Inspector of Taxes on) it will be extremely good
protection for you in the event of a later challenge.

E) 'There is no legal obligation on the taxpayer to keep records
in support of the figures he enters in the (tax return) form.' This
is obviously good practice but you cannot be criticized for not
doing so. Clearly it does not extend to business profits because
the Inspector of Taxes will simply not be satisfied by a single
figure of profit shown in your return and the statement that you
have kept no records. He will probably regard this as a reason for
making exceptionally detailed enquiries and possibly an in-depth
investigation. However, you do not have to keep business records
in the way he would like. Any records will do providing they
will be sufficient to reflect accurately your business profits. A
simple cash book and a simple petty cash book together with
a pile of all the invoices you send out and all the invoices you
have paid is more than enough. (Indeed, to many accountants
dealing with small business records like this would be regarded
as the Holy Grail.) In particular, there is no need to prepare a
balance sheet. The Inspector of Taxes often asks for a balance
sheet but the simple answer is that no balance sheet has been
prepared. He cannot insist on one although if he really wants
one he can make your life a misery until you provide one. If
faced with such a difficulty you should enquire why he thinks
it is so important and what relevance it has to the adequacy of
your profits or any other part of your tax affairs. This will be
enough to stump many Inspectors of Taxes who simply do not
understand what a balance sheet is nor why they asked for it
in the first place, let alone how or why it is prepared.

F) 'If a taxpayer has no knowledge of an item of income or
has been misinformed about it despite having exercised proper

care [the Inland Revenue] would see the resulting omission or understatement as an innocent error.' (Paragraph 19.13). Examples here will be the income of a wife which the husband was not aware of, or interest arising from a bank deposit account which had been opened by mistake by a bank. Invariably the Inland Revenue reject any representation that this is an innocent error and will seek interest and penalties in consequence. Paragraph 19.13. is a very useful arrow in your quiver. Their grounds for taking the cynical view that errors are rarely if ever innocent (except of course where they are in the Inland Revenue's favour) may perhaps be deduced from paragraph 19.1.6. in which they say that if carelessness carried no penalty, the rules would be exploited by the unscrupulous. This reasoning is so obviously faulty that is needs no explanation, but in any event what matters is not that the Inland Revenue would prefer there not to be the concept 'innocent error' but that there is such a concept and while it exists, taxpayers should be given the benefit of it. The Inland Revenue are very fond of saying that they just have to administer the rules and if Parliament has laid down the rules it is too bad if the taxpayer does not like them; they are much less fond of admitting that they should administer the rules just the same when they find the rules not to their liking. It is no business of theirs to make any judgement about the rules at all – their job is not to collect the maximum tax they can screw out of the taxpayer as if they were some commercial organisation being remunerated on a commission basis, but simply to collect the amount which Parliament has laid down as properly payable. This is an important concept and one which can be developed at length, in correspondence if necessary.

This list could go on indefinitely but the above selection illustrates the ammunition available from the Keith Committee report in the event of a challenge by the Inland Revenue. Just think of the effect on an Inspector of Taxes who can be led into making some of the errors outlined above. He may of course go completely wild if you try and get the better of him in this way – but if he does you will be on very strong ground when it comes to making your complaint.

*Chapter Thirteen*

# HOW TO COMPLAIN

# COMPLAINING

If you want to complain about an Inspector of Taxes you must do so with great care. It has been explained in earlier chapters that the taxman has a duty to satisfy himself about the accuracy of your tax return and any business accounts you may send to him, so it is no good complaining that he is doing his statutory duty. You must have more reason than that – earlier chapters have covered some of the circumstances where you might have, or at least be able to make the most of, reasons to complain about the taxman's conduct.

Your first port of call is his boss, the District Inspector. The District Inspector's job is to run the tax office for his district and it is primarily an administrative post. It is a special position, not just one which the oldest man on site ends up with, and the District Inspector will be keen to make sure that his Inspectors do their jobs properly. You should always remember that people tend to complain loudest when they are found out in some wrong-doing (or are about to be found out) and the District Inspector will therefore view complaints about his Inspectors with some scepticism. He will always look at them in this way and only if his Inspector is obviously behaving badly will he intervene to help you. If the taxman is merely acting like a ferret your complaint will look suspect and you can expect no sympathy. So before you complain, make sure that you have a reasonable case and plan how to make the most of it.

Be reasonable, make representations to the Inspector of Taxes and do everything you can to show that he is being unreasonable or prejudicial. Then complain. The chances are that the District Inspector will support the Inspector and say something to the effect that if you do not like it, your remedy is to take your appeal against the assessment to the Commissioners, or if the Inspector has not yet raised an assessment he will ask him to do so so that you can appeal before the Commissioners. This is a plausible line but you should not fall for it. Remember that once an assessment has been raised the taxman does not have to prove that it is right, you have to prove that it is wrong. So if the District Inspector suggests that the answer is to issue an assessment so that you can appeal, you must steer him away from this course. You do not want an assessment, nor the risk of the tax becoming payable, nor the risk of interest being charged, nor the expense of an appeal. What you want is for the taxman to go away and leave you alone. If the District Inspector is not prepared to help you, you must go to the next level which is the Regional Controller. Do not miss this out and go straight to Head Office. Head Office is much more likely to support the District than the Regional Controller who has a wide responsibility for all the districts in his region. But do not expect instant success: indeed it is wise not to expect any success at all.

My first visit to the Regional Controller was extremely instructive in this area and worth retailing because it says a lot about the higher echelons of the Inland Revenue.

I was concerned with a case where the Inspector of Taxes was of the more aggressive type and made all sorts of prejudicial and insulting comments about the taxpayer and generally behaved in a disgraceful manner. The District Inspector was either just as bad, or very weak, and could not adequately control his Inspectors. I was driven to correspond with the Regional Controller and eventually a meeting took place. Now to fully appreciate this story you have to understand that tax offices are places well known for their spartan features. They are soulless places, grey and drab (perhaps all government offices are the same) and the office of the average Inspector of Taxes is very bleak indeed. He has a desk – or something that masquerades as a desk – not wooden but something with a grey plastic top covered in papers, and there are no personal items to be seen such as you would find in any commercial office. There are no curtains, probably not a carpet and the furniture, such as it is, will be little more than functional. He might have a bookcase and a filing cabinet but probably not. The room will be almost empty and it really is the most depressing place in which to work. You are very rarely offered a cup of tea or coffee – if you want one you would need to bring your own mug.

So when I was ushered into the office of the Regional Controller I was in for a real shock. A secretary (a real secretary) showed me the way and I found myself in a room with carpet, expensive-looking blinds on the window, pictures on the wall, a large (wooden) desk and lots of matching furniture including a conference table and chairs in which you could sit with comfort. In short, the type of office you would expect to find occupied by the director of a major company. And when the secretary asked if she could serve tea now, sir, and did so in a china tea service I realized I was in the presence of a bigwig of the highest order. (Looking back I should have guessed because the writing paper upon which his correspondence had been conducted had his name embossed upon it.) A more charming man would be hard to find and of course I got absolutely nowhere. He listened to all my arguments with great courtesy and respect but conceded nothing. I gave it my best shots – the whole works, but still absolutely nothing. He was very impressive indeed and I left feeling that this man was a real professional – the Inland Revenue clearly did not give out offices like that for nothing. I had been given every opportunity to express my grievance in the fullest terms and that was that. Nothing happened – or did it?

Some months later the Inspector of Taxes with whom I was still having my problem left that district and went somewhere else. However, that happens all the time and I could not possibly have attributed his departure to anything I may have said to the Regional Controller, even though the Inspector ended up in a significantly inferior position. I will never know whether I had anything to do with it. The most likely explanation is that mine was not the only complaint and that the powers-that-be decided that demotion was called for anyway. But just possibly my representations had made some difference and they waited for a decent interval before transferring him – but in such a way that I could never claim to have caused it. The moral here is that although you may complain with every justification, the results (if any) may take some time to appear.

If you have been rejected by the District Inspector and the Regional Controller, you can complain to the Board of Inland Revenue at Somerset House. Even if you receive another rebuff, you are not finished. There is always the Ombudsman.

## The Ombudsman

The Ombudsman, or to give him his proper title, The Parliamentary Commissioner for Administration, really is your last resort. His power is very limited (indeed there is a good case for saying that he has no power at all) and many people complain to the Ombudsman without any understanding of his function or what he can do to help – which is often very little.

The purpose of the Ombudsman is to investigate claims of maladministration by government departments. You cannot apply to him directly but only through your MP who will refer your complaint to him – but usually only after the MP has made some effort on your behalf to resolve the problem. The Ombudsman will look into your complaint in private and has considerable powers to enable him to do so. He can call for the production of any documents he requires (except Cabinet papers) and can call civil servants to an interview if he chooses. He is not bound to look into your complaint – he has full discretion and will not investigate unmeritorious or vexatious cases. More importantly he will not do anything if you have a legal remedy (for example the opportunity of an appeal) still available to you. If therefore you are in dispute with the taxman you can forget the Ombudsman because you can still take your appeal to the Commissioners for an independent hearing. He might just step in if you are being unfairly pressurized out of your proper remedy by the threat of costs but that is most unusual and unlikely.

The most important point to appreciate is that the Ombudsman is only concerned with maladministration which covers bias, neglect, inattention, delay, incompetence, ineptitude, perversity, turpitude, and arbitrariness. Unless you can show one of these failings on the part of the Inland Revenue, and that you have exhausted all available legal remedies, the Ombudsman will not be of much help to you. An example of where the Ombudsman is often involved would be unreasonable delays in the dealing with correspondence or claims for repayment of tax. In such cases there is no available remedy – all you can do is complain and if your representations elsewhere have not been effective the Ombudsman will be able to step in. I say 'step in' but even if he finds that there has been maladministration, you will be disappointed to discover that he has no power to do anything about it. All he can do is to make a report to Parliament and to recommend that the matter is put right. Fortunately the Inland Revenue are fairly sensitive about their image these days and will in most cases implement his recommendations – often with a surprisingly good grace.

Any application to the Ombudsman will inevitably take a long time and there can be no guarantee that anything will happen as a result. However it is a last resort and there is nothing to be lost in the attempt – provided of course that you do satisfy the relevant conditions. It is also a worthwhile threat to make to the taxman if things have gone badly wrong with his handling of your affairs. But do not mention it too early because the taxman will ignore you. He will know the extent to which he is at risk from such an approach and will ignore you if your threat is ill-founded or premature. If you wait until the right time and demonstrate that you are aware of the right procedure, he will be much more impressed and likely to respond more helpfully.

*Chapter Fourteen*

# THE SPECIAL PROBLEMS OF THE SELF-EMPLOYED

# THE SELF-EMPLOYED

The Inland Revenue have concentrated very heavily in recent years on the tax affairs of the self-employed and have on numerous occasions selected whole industries for an in-depth review; they then apply their conclusions indiscriminately across the board. Large numbers of people who are self-employed have suffered as a result of the Inland Revenue's attention in this area and people who engage others on a self-employed basis have not escaped either. Accordingly the whole subject of self-employment and the self-employed is worthy of considerable explanation. Furthermore as the Inland Revenue's approach is often open to criticism it is by no means beyond being successfully challenged. On the other hand you may inadvertently be dealing with these matters incorrectly and you could be building up real trouble – and the longer you leave it the more expensive it may become.

You may feel that you would like to be self-employed because of all the tax advantages which go with it, rather than being employed and taxed under PAYE. It is well known that you can claim a tax deduction for many more expenses if you are self-employed and also the National Insurance contributions are much lower. Conversely you may want somebody to do some work for you and would much rather pay them on a self-employed basis, leaving them to pay their own tax and National Insurance contributions. Not only would you save approximately 10 per cent which is the amount of the employer's N.I.C. but you would not have to deduct tax either – and deducting tax is not a good incentive to getting somebody to do some work for you.

These are perfectly legitimate aims but not as easily achieved as you may think. If you are going to succeed, you do need to know what you are doing, and the implications. It is not enough just to say that you are working as a self-employed person; self-serving declarations are of little value on their own. Whether or not you are self-employed (and therefore whether you will be allowed the tax advantages) is a matter of law and will depend upon a number of different tests which are explained below. The taxman is aware of the advantages and will therefore be arguing to the contrary so if you want to be treated as self-employed you have to satisfy as many of the tests as possible.

## The Relevant Tests

It is often easy to distinguish between a person who is employed (such as an apprentice) and one who is self-employed (such as an architect in private practice). However, there are many people whose working arrangements are more difficult to classify and you may well be in this grey area – or at least the Inland Revenue will say that you are. Therefore you must examine all the relevant criteria to identify the correct position.

In broad terms it needs to be determined whether the person doing the work is the servant of the person for whom the work is done, or more accurately whether the work is undertaken under a contract of employment known as a 'Contract of Service' or as a self-employed person working as an independent contractor under a 'Contract for Services'. These terms ought to be known because they are used widely by the Inland Revenue. You do not have to use them, but if you do, make sure that you do not mix them up during your argument or you will put yourself at a considerable disadvantage indicating that you do not really understand the distinction between them.

There is no single test which can be appled to determine whether you are employed or self-employed, nor unfortunately is there an exhaustive list; furthermore there are no strict rules about how much weight should be given to one factor rather than another. This may sound incredibly vague and unhelpful, but it is not nearly as imprecise as it appears. What you have to do is to look at all the relevant criteria and to make a judgement about which side of the line your circumstances fall. However, you should remember that you need to weigh the factors in the balance and if most of them are neutral, that is they give no clear indication one way or another, one single factor pointing firmly in the right direction could end up being conclusive.

In this area perhaps more than any other there are decided cases to support every point of view and you should not be discouraged by the taxman quoting a precedent which seems to destroy your argument entirely. There will usually be another case which supports your view and probably with equal strength. It would be as well for you to find it (a good reference book would have all the decided cases for you to look through) but if you cannot, it is quite reasonable for you to say to the taxman that you have no intention of trading case authorities with him because there are numerous conflicting cases supporting each side and every case depends on its own facts. If you feel particularly confident you could well suggest to the taxman that in the interests of reaching the correct conclusion he ought to point to all the cases which are against him as well as the cases which support his view; after all barristers appearing in court must draw the court's attention to cases both for and against their arguments (they have a positive professional duty to do so) and that this honourable rule should be equally applicable in a more modest legal dispute.

## *Control*

The element of control is a highly relevant factor; the essential nature of a servant is that he obeys all the reasonable directions of his master. In any contract where one person agrees to do something for another person in return for payment there will invariably exist an element of control because the person doing the work will want to give satisfaction, and the person paying will want to be satisfied. The amount of control will obviously vary from case to case but what is important is the degree of control over what is to be done and how, when and where the tasks are to be performed.

In the world of the performing arts the individual will in some respects be beyond the control of the management. It will be his own personality and abilities which will make or mar him as an artiste. No matter how much he may be directed or instructed, it will be his natural talents that count. However, such a person is not necessarily precluded from being an employee if all the elements of control within the competence of the management are exercised; but these things really only confuse the issue and the legal relationship between the parties is more likely to be determined by other factors.

The taxman tends to go overboard on the control test, often ignoring everything else, so it is important to draw to his attention that control is just one of the factors to be weighed in the balance. In one famous case on this subject the judge said that 'control is not everything' and this quotation can be very very useful if the taxman gets carried away. However, it is not a bad idea to encourage the taxman to rely only on control and to ignore everything else because if everything else points in favour of your argument, the element of control will cease to be particularly relevant. So great is their preoccupation with control that this ploy has a very high chance of success.

## Exclusivity

This is another test beloved of the taxman. Where one person works exclusively for another there is usually a presumption that he is an employee, if only because the provision of exclusive services is consistent with an employment. However, this can lead to a false conclusion because exclusivity may be nothing more than the inevitable consequence of the amount of work needing to be done, leaving no time (or possibly inclination) for work to be undertaken for anybody else. What is more important is whether the person is free to work for others should he choose to do so.

Where there is an exclusive contract prohibiting work for another person the presumption of an employment is increased; this aspect overlaps with considerations regarding control because if one person is under exclusive contract to another a degree of control may well exist and this will enhance the Inland Revenue's argument in support of an employment. If you undertake work for two persons at the same time particularly in the same field, this is an indication that you are self-employed and carrying on business on your own account, because these facts are inconsistent with the terms of an employment with either party. The denial of exclusivity here also denies control and goes some way to supporting the other tests for self-employment.

Accordingly if you are in doubt about your self-employed status you should make quite sure that you work for more than one person at the same time. This is helpful but not conclusive because it is quite possible for a person to have two part-time employments – a great deal would depend upon the terms on which the work is done and this inevitably brings in the other tests.

It can be argued, and if you are challenged you should argue, that the performance of every service has to be exclusive to a certain extent because you cannot generally do two things at exactly the same time. This prevents the taxman dragging too much out of the exclusivity argument. The question is how long a service needs to be performed before it is regarded as sufficiently exclusive to indicate an employment. It has to be considered sensibly whether on balance, the degree of exclusivity combined with the other factors are more indicative of an employment or otherwise.

Do not bother with separate agreements or a series of separate agreements each time work is to be performed. Nobody will take much notice and in any event the agreements might do nothing more than indicate a series of short employments. Do not be bludgeoned by the Inland Revenue into agreeing that if you are employed in one capacity you cannot be self-employed in another – just think of doctors employed part-time by the National Health Service who carry on a private practice. There is no special rule which applies for doctors and this example is enough to confound any such suggestion by the Inland Revenue.

## Mutual Understandings and Obligations

This is one of the most important tests but the Inland Revenue nearly always try to ignore it – usually because it is rarely helpful to their point of view. It is in fact the contractual background to the relationship between the parties. Are you an independent principal or are you in a master/servant relationship? If the parties knowingly enter into an agreement for work to be done on the specific basis that the worker is not to be an employee, it is impossible for the Inland Revenue completely to ignore this and say that because they do not think much of such a contract they can charge tax on the basis of some quite different contract which neither of the parties entered into. All they can do is to say that the true relationship between the parties is one of master and servant and although the parties thought they were entering into some other contract the proper legal analysis of their agreement is an employment. This is a very tall order for the Inland Revenue and they usually try to avoid it by ignoring the contractual position altogether. You must therefore stuff it down their throats and make them address the point; they should not in all conscience object because they should not be attempting to win the argument at all costs, but merely trying to determine the proper position.

It is important to appreciate that self-imposed labels do very little good. However, they are better than nothing. It is better to say that you are self-employed than not to say so because it could just tip the balance. Generally if the facts show that you are self-employed, you do not need a label, and if they show the

reverse, a label will not help you. From earlier chapters you will
have gathered that the idea is to present a good arguable case
sufficient to deter the Inland Revenue from taking the matter
seriously to appeal, and if you have enough of the above factors
on your side and a label supporting your view, it might just mean
the difference between success and failure. If pushed you can
reasonably argue that if both parties consider the relationship
is one of independent principals and there is nothing in the
realities of the situation which actually conflicts with this statement, the Inland Revenue are bound to accept it. They will not
necessarily agree but it is a very powerful point for you to make.

Another contractual point is that if you have a master/servant
relationship there are also mutual obligations – on the employer
to offer work and on the employee to perform it. If these mutual
obligations do not exist there simply cannot be an employment
as a matter of law. And it is law which we are dealing with.
This is extremely important and you should always think about
it carefully before starting work, because if you can set this up
from the beginning, the Inland Revenue will always have an
uphill struggle. Unfortunately, you lose the initiative here if you
do not set the scene from the outset because then the obligations
have to be (and invariably will be) inferred from the conduct of
the parties.

It is sometimes thought to be a good idea to have a written
agreement to prove that you are self-employed. Unless this is
done with great skill it is something definitely to be avoided.
Most written agreements created for this purpose do more harm
than good. They can also lack credibility. When the plumber
comes to mend your pipes, or the window cleaner comes to clean
your windows, you do not enter into a detailed written contract
explaining that you do not regard him as your employee and that
he will not be entitled to holiday etc. The very idea is absurd
and if you did so even in less absurd circumstances it would
probably be counter-productive, in that it might encourage the
Inland Revenue to draw the opposite conclusion.


## Payment

The method of payment for the work will always provide
some indication of whether or not an employment exists. If
the payment is expressed in terms which normally apply to an

employment e.g. wages or salaries, this will of course suggest an employment. However, this should not be given undue weight because you will probably be able to say that this is simply a convenient shorthand and not an accurate description. A more appropriate test would be to consider how the payment ought properly to be described objectively.

Regularity of payment can indicate an employment because again this is a method by which employees are generally paid. However, this may be no more than good commercial practice. Many self-employed people arrange for their fees to be paid regularly at fixed amounts by standing order and this does not give rise to any adverse inference.

The factors which determine the amount paid may also be highly relevant. Employees generally receive payments by reference to hours of attendance and payment cannot usually be withheld if the services are unsatisfactory. On the other hand, where payment is dependent upon the adequacy of the services performed, this would be indicative of self-employment. The payment of a fixed fee does nothing to damage the argument for self-employment because by doing the work efficiently in a shorter time the individual will be able to profit from his own efficiency by using the time saved to his own advantage.

Calculating the amount of payment by reference to hours worked can rarely be an indication either way as many self-employed persons charge a fee based on an hourly or daily rate. Similarly the payment of overtime may not be much more of an indication either because long hours will generally demand a premium rate – time and a half perhaps when an employee, or an uplifted fee in the case of a self-employed person.

One important characteristic of the self-employed person is that he will generally be paid more than an employee would be paid for doing the same work. This is because a self-employed person would usually be required to work only on a specific assignment and the payer would not have to pay for time when the person's services are not required – nor would he be liable for the additional costs associated with office facilities and NIC. If you can establish comparative rates of pay demonstrating that you receive a higher level of remuneration this can be powerful evidence in support of self employment.

The regular payment of expenses to an individual in connection with his work is generally consistent with an employment, although some self-employed persons do include expenses on their invoices. Do not despair if you are paid expenses agreed in advance to be in accordance with the scale of expenses payable to employees generally, because this may merely be a matter of administrative or political convenience for the payer, so that his employees do not become dissatisfied with their regular expenses. You would be well advised to submit an invoice covering all fees and disbursements (and VAT if you are registered) because this will represent evidence that you are in business on your own account. However, invoices are often not submitted, particularly by those not registered for VAT, and it should therefore be made clear from the outset whether the amounts receivable for the work are gross amounts, with the recipient being responsible for his own tax and NIC, or whether the payments are net of all deductions. This is an area where confusion often arises and it is wise for the respective obligations to be settled in advance.

In the field of entertainment it can be of particular relevance to establish who possesses the copyright and other fruits of the work undertaken. If the individual is employed these rights will invariably belong to the employer but if the individual is self-employed the rights will generally belong to him. That is not to say that an employer cannot relinquish his rights in favour of an employee but this would be comparatively unusual. An agreement that the copyright belongs to the individual would be much more consistent with self employment. Similarly the rights for screen or publishing credits would indicate a self employment because this gives support to the argument that the individual is in business on his own account. If he arranges for publicity to be given to him for his work this will clearly enhance his reputation thereby enabling him to profit from the good management of his business affairs. This may seem a trivial point but you may need every bit of support for your arguments.

### Place of Work

The place where the work is carried out can be helpful in identifying which type of contract exists; obviously if the work is carried out at the client's premises and office facilities are provided by him this will be more consistent with an employment than otherwise. Furthermore, the regular presence of the individual at the premises will enhance the ability for control to be exercised and limit any opportunity for working elsewhere. He would look like an employee and may appear to be 'part and parcel' of the employer's organisation which can be disadvantageous – see below. If the place where the services are to be performed is specified in the contract this would add further weight to the taxman's argument that an employment exists. However, you should not let the taxman go overboard on this argument. It may be that the work is done at the client's premises simply because the individual finds it the most convenient location or perhaps because it is absolutely necessary. For example, a freelance landscape gardener can hardly be expected to perform his services anywhere other than in the garden he is landscaping.

## Provision of Equipment

Who provides the equipment for the work may also be relevant. Generally an employer will tend to provide all necessary equipment and facilities for his employees and a self-employed person will tend to provide his own or at least to have the right to specify which equipment is to be used. However, this is not an invariable rule and it would depend upon the nature of the work involved. A skilled carpenter will nearly always provide his own tools whether he is employed or not because his tools will be of special significance to him. In this circumstance the provision of equipment does nothing to indicate the nature of the relationship either way. Conversely, a self-employed concert pianist would usually be provided with the necessary equipment to use in his performance; he would not be expected to take his own piano and piano stool to each venue where he is invited to play. These examples can be very useful if the Inland Revenue suggest that the provision of equipment is relevant in your circumstances, because they show the weakness of the point he is trying to make.

## Personal Services

A Contract of Service by definition involves personal service by the employee. It is sometimes suggested by the Inland Revenue that where the services of a particular person are required, this indicates an employment – but this is a poor point. The best that can be said is that if the individual is not obliged to perform the work himself and can arrange for the work to be performed by a substitute or a subordinate, this would indicate self-employment services because these are factors wholly inconsistent with an employment. Many self-employed individuals have a special area of expertise and their particular skills may be sought on a consultancy basis. Obviously personal service would be an essential ingredient because the client pays for the skill of that particular person (e.g. leading counsel) and it would be absurd to suggest that this means he is necessarily an employee.

It should always be argued that where a personal service is not an essential ingredient in the contract, a contract of employment cannot exist, whereas where personal service is required the position can only be neutral and the relationship between the parties has to be determined by reference to other tests. This is a useful factor to have under your belt because at best it is supportive to your argument and at worst it does not help the taxman's argument.

## Part and Parcel

The Inland Revenue often suggests that a relevant test for determining the relationship between the parties is whether the person is 'part and parcel' of the employer's organisation. There was some authority for this view which the Inland Revenue used to trot out, but it has now become discredited and you should be able to demolish any such suggestion without too much trouble. Furthermore, commonsense tells you that whether a person is part and parcel of an organisation is simply a question of appearance and it is wholly wrong to say that the true nature of a contractual relationship can be determined by how it appears to somebody else. The third party may be well (or ill) informed but his opinion can hardly be used as evidence of a relationship between two other people.

It is quite possible that the skills of the self-employed person are so valuable that he is constantly involved in the important parts of the business (perhaps as a consultant or other adviser) so that he could reasonably be regarded as an indispensable part of the proper functioning of the business; thus he might be regarded as part and parcel of the organisation by a third party but that is entirely irrelevant. The test is whether the person in this position is capable of exercising executive power; this would indicate actual authority within the business consistent with an employment. Where there is no executive power it is difficult for the Inland Revenue sensibly to argue that an employment exists.

## In Business on your own Account

Several references have been made above to whether or not an individual is in business on his own account. This is an important test but it is really no more than a conclusion to be drawn from the other tests and from the work which is involved. If you maintain your own books and records, deal with your own financial affairs, make your own arrangements for business insurances, issue invoices and are registered for VAT, a business would clearly be indicated; similarly an absence of these factors may indicate that no real business is being carried on. The existence of secretarial assistance, even from the spouse, or of an agent engaged to find work will obviously be points in favour of self-employed status. However, you still have to demonstrate that you are free to run your business as you see fit, however modest it may be, even though you may be constrained by the requirements of your clients.

Another extremely helpful point in this context is whether the individual has the opportunity to profit from the sound management of his business. This is an important test and is often given insufficient weight by the Inland Revenue. The self-employed person can profit from sound management of his business by working efficiently and completing any given assignment early – provided of course that he can go home afterwards. This may not increase the amount of payment receivable but it will give him more time to do other work or to deal with other aspects of his business.

Where he is responsible for the administrative arrangements concerning the receipt of income and payment of expenses relating to his work, he will have the opportunity to manage his cash flow and perhaps minimize his bank interest, thereby profiting from the sound management of his business.

An extension of this point, which is rarely appreciated by the Inland Revenue without explanation, is that it is relevant to consider the converse position whereby the individual can suffer financially be conducting his business affairs badly. The opportunity of making a loss is generally denied to an employee whose salary will be paid almost irrespective of his foolish conduct – although he might lose his job. If the person performing the work can suffer financially as a result of poor performance e.g. by not being paid for his work, this will be powerful evidence in support of self-employment.

An employee will generally not have to risk his own capital in connection with his work. The absence of any financial risk by an individual is consistent with an employment but it has to be borne in mind that many activities, particularly those involved in services, do not involve much financial commitment and accordingly the amount of financial risk may be very small – possibly extending only to the risk of legal action for negligent work. However, where this risk exists self employment will be strongly indicated, but the taxman will not appreciate this point unless you make it very clear to him.

Other financial risks occur which are worthy of being brought out in the correspondence. An employee has financial security because he is protected by his contract of employment and all the benefits of the Employment Protection Acts giving him rights of considerable value. A self-employed person has no such protection – he has the right to be paid for the proper performance of his assignment and nothing more. Sometimes he does not even get paid because there is always a risk of a bad debt. Furthermore if the work is unsatisfactory he may have to correct it at his own expense. This lack of financial security represents a genuine financial risk and it must be brought clearly to the attention of the Inland Revenue.

Finally on this aspect, it is not unusual to find self-employed people who find it difficult to deal efficiently with their tax affairs; a lack of attention to this part of their business can give rise to a considerable degree of financial risk, not least because it may expose them to monetary tax penalties (explained in Chapter 9) and that is a real financial risk which the taxman ought to have no difficulty in understanding.

## Termination

The method by which the contract (whether it is in writing or not) can be terminated will give you some indication of the true nature of the contract. A crucial feature in connection with the terms of the contract is whether it can be assigned to a third party. If the benefit of the contract can be assigned this will strongly indicate a Contract for Services, because an employment contract is incapable of assignment. Even a term in the contract precluding assignment would indicate a self employment because such a terms would be entirely unnecessary in a contract of employment.

## Department of Social Security

You may think that because the DSS treat you as self-employed that ought to be enough to convince the Inland Revenue; unfortunately it is not. The Inland Revenue tend to say that the tax position is different and to ignore the DSS position entirely. They are wrong to do so and you should tell them so in firm terms because if you look at all the decided cases which the Inland Revenue will put forward to say that you are really an employee, you will find that most of them are cases based on national insurance matters.

There is however a strange practice whereby the DSS will treat some people as being employees (so that they can claim unemployment benefit) while the Inland Revenue will treat them as self-employed. There are many examples of this in the entertainment industry. This is quite simply an administrative practice based on nothing but convenience of the government departments and you should not allow it to be used against you.

## The Implications

A person who claims to be paying somebody on a self-employed basis takes a considerable risk – indeed nearly all the risks are on his side. If he is right there is no problem but if he is wrong and the Inland Revenue challenge the position he will be in real difficulty. He can ask the Inland Revenue to collect the tax from the other person but (with one exception) it will not get him anywhere. There is a legal obligation to deduct tax under PAYE from payments to employees and if you fail to do so the Inland Revenue will make you pay the amount which should have been deducted – so that you end up seriously out of pocket. And they might charge interest and penalties.

How then do you protect yourself? The first thing to do is to appreciate the danger and take the matter seriously. You can try to deduct the tax and hold on to it just in case, but that is not likely to go down very well. You should therefore make sure that the person to whom you are paying the money gross really is self-employed, and at the very least get a statement from him that if you end up having to pay the tax to the Inland Revenue, he will reimburse you. At least this gets over the familiar problem of him later claiming that he thought he was being paid net of tax and that you had already deducted tax before paying him.

By far the best course of actions is to run through all the above tests and agree with him that on all counts he should be properly regarded as self-employed. Examine all areas of doubt and think of some good reasons why those doubts should be resolved in your favour. If possible ask him for a letter from his accountant confirming that he is taxed under schedule D, and if he does not have one ask him for his tax reference number. (If he does not have a tax reference number you are mad to pay him gross.) If he gives you his tax reference number you can tell whether it is a schedule D or a schedule E reference by the number of the digits. If it is a 3 digit number followed by a 5 digit number eg. 123/12345, it will be a self-employed reference and you can relax. If in doubt ring up the Inland Revenue and ask whether or not it is a PAYE or a schedule D district.

What this does for you is provide you with a reasonable excuse and you might find yourself wanting one of these quite badly. The PAYE regulations (and in particular regulation 26) provide that if you pay the other person gross by reason of a genuine error made in good faith, the Inland Revenue will leave you alone and will chase him for the tax on the earnings. But to succeed with this excuse it must be a genuine error made in good faith – so you need to show that you took all reasonable care to establish the correct position. The taxman will often say that if you are in any doubt you should have consulted the tax office and the fact that you have not done so is conclusive evidence against you. This a good example of the Inland Revenue's penchant for circular arguments. You must therefore be in no doubt – you must be clear in your own mind that self-employment was the correct treatment by reference to the above tests.

It is not helpful to say that you cannot remember the name

of the person you paid. This will be a clear indication that you did not take your obligations seriously and the Inland Revenue will insist on you paying the tax. Alternatively they might say that without better evidence you cannot claim a tax deduction for the amounts paid and this can make the exercise much more expensive than if you paid the tax in the first place.

Whenever the question of self employment is raised by the Inland Revenue you should be on your guard and look very carefully at the above tests. If you lose one of these arguments it can be very expensive, because the taxman will invariably want to go back and reopen earlier years. You can only head him off by either winning the argument or by showing that even if he is right you had a reasonable excuse. Each alternative requires you to have taken careful steps from the beginning and if you have been a little casual in this area in the past you should immediately tighten up your procedures so that if an enquiry is made you will be seen in the best possible light.

*Chapter Fifteen*

# INHERITANCE TAX

# INHERITANCE TAX

Inheritance tax is the latest name for death duties. For nearly a century there was a tax on death called Estate Duty but in 1975 a whole new system was introduced not only for charging tax on a person's death, but also taxing gifts made during lifetime. This was called Capital Transfer Tax. In 1986 there was some important changes which brought back some of the old Estate Duty rules and amalgamated them with Capital Transfer Tax. They called this combination Inheritance Tax. The amalgamation has not been very successful and it has caused a lot of unnecessary technical difficulties but that is not a matter which is particularly important here. The rates of tax are changed regularly and at the present time there is a single flat rate of Inheritance Tax of 40 per cent (20 per cent for chargeable lifetime gifts) over £118,000 – the first £118,000 is tax free and known as the nil band.

The first thing you need to know when planning to save inheritance tax is that this tax is not dealt with by Inspectors of Taxes in tax offices – it is dealt with by an entirely separate office known as the Capital Taxes office which is in the same building and is closely related to the Inland Revenue Shares Valuation Division (see chapter 16). That is not particularly significant in itself – except for the fact that the Capital Taxes office deals with nothing but inheritance tax, so the correspondence tends to be of rather a higher standard than normal. However, just because they can (and do) engage in complex analysis of the inheritance tax rules in heavy technical language, does not mean that they get it right. Sometimes they do, sometimes they don't – but unfortunately you will not be able to tell the difference. A technical debate with the Capital Taxes office is not recommended, because they will leave you for dead unless you have a really good knowledge of the technical inheritance tax rules. This is an area where professional help is definitely required, but not only for this reason; in all problems associated with inheritance tax the sums involved tend to be rather high and if you are dealing with large sums of money, the cost of professional advice becomes more worthwhile.

You are unlikely to come across inheritance tax problems by accident. The Capital Taxes office do not carry out investigations like the other branches of the Inland Revenue; they tend only to react when you tell them something – and not always even then. However, that does not mean that they are above charging you interest and penalties if you get things wrong. The most usual difficulty with inheritance tax planning is that it simply does not work i.e. you do something in the expectation that it will save you inheritance tax on your death, and it doesn't. The trouble here is that you never find out but those you leave behind will do so, and will have to pick up the pieces. Worse still, you can actually end up doubling or tripling your inheritance tax liability by getting your plans wrong. With this as a real possibility you must make quite sure that your plans do work and this is every bit as difficult as it sounds.

A few brief words of explanation about the tax may be helpful here. Inheritance tax is based on 'transfers of value' of which there are three main types: chargeable transfers, potentially exempt transfers and exempt transfers.

Chargeable transfers are those which give rise to an immediate charge to tax and generally take place on death (when the whole estate comes into charge) or on some lifetime gifts – mainly gifts into discretionary trusts. A discretionary trust is one where the trustees have a discretion over which of a number of beneficiaries are to receive benefits from the trust fund. No beneficiary has any entitlement to anything from such a trust, merely the right to be considered by the trustees as a possible object of the exercise of their discretion. This is to be distinguished from a fixed interest trust where a specific beneficiary has an entitlement to part of the trust fund, perhaps only the income; gifts to such fixed interest trusts are treated as potentially exempt transfers.

Potentially exempt transfers are gifts which are made more than seven years before death between individuals. This means that when you make a gift it is presumed to be exempt and no tax is chargeable, provided that you survive for seven years. If you do not survive for seven years the gifts become chargeable. Hence they are called potentially exempt transfers. During this seven-year period there is a tapering relief so that if you die in the 4th, 5th, 6th, or 7th year from the date of the gift, the amount charged will go down in stages by 20 per cent; if therefore you die within three years of making the gift the whole amount will be chargeable whereas if you die in the 4th year only 80 per cent of the gift will be charged, in the 5th year only 60 per cent and so on.

Exempt transfers are gifts (including those on death) to which some specific exemption applies. The most widely known exemptions are those for gifts between spouses and gifts up to £3,000 per annum.

As mentioned above, inheritance tax is too complex a subject to enable any particular tax saving device to be seriously examined – anyway that is not the purpose of this book. The aim here is to warn of trouble on the horizon so that you can steer clear of difficulty, and to point to areas where you may be able to gain an advantage.

## *Potentially Exempt Transfers*

When you make a gift which qualifies as a potentially exempt transfer there is no need to tell the taxman. This sounds like an advantage because you do not have to be bothered with filling in forms (or worry about penalties for not doing so); however this rule can be extremely irritating if you want to know the amount of the gift you have made at the time. This will not matter if your gift is cash, or something with a fixed or easily ascertained value, but if your gift is shares in the family company (and it so often is) you will not be able even to guess at the value which will be transferred by the potentially exempt transfer. Why on earth should you want to know? One good reason is so that you can calculate the risk you are taking with the potential liability. If you die within seven years the P.E.T. will become a chargeable transfer and the value which will be taxed is not the value of the subject matter at the date of death, but the value at the date of the actual transfer. So if you are a little worried about this potential liability in the event of an untimely death during this period and want to insure against it by term assurance (which is very inexpensive) you do want to know what amount to insure against. Furthermore, if you have in mind making more than one gift during your lifetime you will not know the value of the previous gifts made in the previous seven years. Therefore if you are trying to do any planning at all, it is rather important to know the value of the gift that you are making. Unfortunately the taxman will not help you. He will say that his job is to value transfers for the purposes of establishing a tax liability – not to assist you in planning to avoid the tax. Accordingly he will only be interested if the gift you make gives rise to some tax; P.E.T.s do not give rise to any tax at the time they are made so he will only turn his mind to the value when and if it becomes necessary. Try as you might he will not help you, and you therefore have to arrange matters slightly differently; what you have to do is not make a P.E.T. but a chargeable transfer. At this point you may feel the need to ask for some professional help because everything starts becoming rather technical. Your professional adviser will know that a chargeable transfer is immediately chargeable and the taxman is obliged to value the transfer to see whether any tax arises. Unfortunately he can still frustrate you; he might say that because the first £118,000 of chargeable transfers do not give rise to any tax as they do not exceed the nil rate band, all he needs to do is to satisfy himself that your transfer does not exceed this value. So he still does not have to value your gift – he just has to say that this is not large enough to give rise to any tax. Admittedly he has effectively put a ceiling on the value of your transfer of £118,000 – but if you think that the shares in your family company may be worth something between £50,000 and £100,000, this is not helping very much. You must therefore make your gift or gifts large enough to give rise to some real tax because then you can be sure of establishing a value. The tax does not have to be very much, just a few hundred pounds or so, but enough to serve the purpose.

It will almost certainly be necessary to use a discretionary trust because the only chargeable transfer you are likely to make is a transfer into such a trust; all the following references to chargeable transfers are therefore assumed to be of this nature. Chargeable transfers are chargeable at only half the rate which applies on death so if you make a chargeable transfer or transfers of £120,000 (assuming that you have fully utilised your annual exemptions) the tax would be only £400 calculated as under:

| | |
|---|---|
| Chargeable transfer | £120,000 |
| Nil rate band | £118,000 |
| | |
| Amount chargeable | £  2,000 |
| | |
| Inheritance tax at 20% | £    400 |

However, arranging a gift of exactly £120,000 is not too easy because it is rather precise and the whole point is that you do not know the precise value – indeed that is exactly what you are trying to find out. If you have in mind giving away some shares in your family company, you have to do it in stages. The first step is to settle a small parcel of shares on discretionary trusts; this will create the first chargeable transfer and you can see what the taxman says. He will inevitably say that it falls below £118,000. Then you do it again. You will probably get the same answer. The taxman has now effectively agreed that each parcel is worth no more than £59,000. So you do it again and again (preferably with smaller and smaller parcels) and eventually you will end up going past the £118,000 threshold. Naturally do not just accept the taxman's valuation; argue at each stage that the value of each transfer is extremely low so that you can get more transfers in before going over the limit. When you do go over the limit you will be able to get into a full scale negotiation on the share value with all guns blazing to ensure that the real tax is kept to absolute minimum.

You may find that the taxman does not like you doing this, but it is really no business of his if you choose to make gifts in this way. He may try to be awkward and value the second or third gifts very highly – and that is exactly what you want him to do. You want to get into negotiations over value so that you know where you are. However, he might seek to reopen his previous views about earlier transfers and this is something you should guard against from the outset with great care. At each stage you ascertain from him a specific assurance that the value of transfers to date do not exceed £118,000. He may wriggle, but you must force it out of him. It would be a breach of his public duty for him to say (and he will therefore never do so) that he does not want to value your gift. If there is a tax liability which arises depending upon the value of the gift he has a duty to determine it and to cause the tax to be collected. He cannot say that he cannot be bothered. All he can do is to say that he is satisfied that no tax liability arises. So you must not be fobbed off with 'a provisional view' or 'at the present time it seems' or any similarly vague expression. What he must mean is that the values do not exceed £118,000. You should ask him to confirm it and if he will not, ask him what it does mean. There really is no avoiding this obligation and you should stick with it until he gives you the answer you want, although most of the time it will not be necessary.

## Reservations of Benefit

The first priority in making a gift with a view to saving inheritance tax is to avoid doing anything which will actually increase your inheritance tax liability. Nothing could be more daft and there are few things more beloved by a tax adviser than the layman who does a bit of planning of his own and in his ignorance falls down a big hole. The fee for digging him out is always going to be high – and hardly a matter for complaint by the client; furthermore it gives the client a really good lesson why professional advice is expensive. All in all, it is mighty good for fee generation. To understand how this can happen you must know about a central principle of inheritance tax planning which is the concept of the 'reservation of a benefit'.

If you make a gift but reserve any benefit or enjoyment from the subject matter of the gift you are wasting your time because the taxman will treat the asset as remaining in your estate if you die. An obvious example would be to give away your house to your children but remain in occupation. The continued occupation is the clearest possible reservation of a benefit and if you die you will still be taxed as if you owned the house, no matter how long has elapsed since you made the gift. The seven-year period does not start to run until your benefit ceases. You may say that this is not so bad – you have just wasted your time and failed to get the tax advantage you hoped for; unfortunately the position is much worse than that. You did actually make the gift and this will not be ignored, so if you die within seven years it will be counted as a previous transfer. If your house was worth £250,000, the gift to your children will be treated as a gift of that value which will be counted as part of your life time transfers if you die within seven years. So if you die within three years you have a cumulative total of life time gifts of £250,000 and your estate on your death (i.e. the house) will be £250,000 so you will be taxed on death as if your estate were really £500,000. The tax will be £150,000 whereas if you had done nothing at all it would only have been £50,000; you have increased the inheritance tax liability on your death by £100,000. That is really good planning! There are some special provisions which provide relief against double charges and these would apply to such a simple case – but the reliefs are complex and if your arrangements are not quite so simple it is easy to find yourself outside the terms of the relief.

To make a gift without a reservation of benefit is not easy; you have to know the rules really well because a reservation of benefit can arise in the most obscure fashion. For example if you run a company and give away some shares to your son, the fact that you remain a director or an employee of the company can represent the reservation of a benefit. The same applies if you take your son into partnership with you. Some positive steps have to be taken to prevent the special rule applying in these circumstances. You might think that another alternative would be to put some money into trust for your children or grandchildren and to make sure that the trust deed states that under no circumstances can you ever become entitled to any benefit from the settlement. Surely this would do? Unfortunately it may not because unless the trust is very carefully drawn up you could find the Inland Revenue saying that a resulting trust could arise or that some power of resettlement contained within the deed could override the express exclusion. This is straying into highly technical areas but these possibilities are mentioned just to show the lengths that the Inland Revenue will go to find a reserved benefit in respect of any gift. If they can find a reservation of a benefit they can undo all your inheritance tax planning so they are bound to be on the lookout.

## Capital Gains Tax

Another real trap where you can accidentally increase your tax liabilities arises in connection with Capital Gains Tax. When you die, all your assets are revalued for Capital Gains Tax purposes without charge; there is of course a charge to Inheritance Tax unless some exemption arises but your family takes over the assets at a new (and much higher) base value for Capital Gains Tax. If therefore your business is worth £300,000 which you started from scratch ten years ago you might want to pass it over to your son during your lifetime; this would enable him to carry on the business without the worry of Inheritance Tax arising if you had waited until you died before passing the business to him. This will be a P.E.T. and no charge would arise if you survive for seven years. No Capital Gains Tax need arise either because you can make a claim for your son to be treated as having acquired the business for Capital Gains Tax purposes at your original acquisition cost. This is obviously a sound arrangement and one which is being undertaken all the time up and down the country. Consider, however, the position if you were to die within three years. Your potentially exempt transfer would become chargeable and you would therefore save no Inheritance Tax at all, but because you did not own the business at your death there is no Capital Gains Tax free uplift. This may not matter a great deal if your son intends to carry on the business permanently (in that case there will never be a disposal by him and the Capital Gains Tax would never arise) but if, for example, he decides to sell the business (or indeed if he feels it is necessary to do so to pay the inheritance) he will have to pay the Capital Gains Tax as well. He will therefore get the worst of all worlds and most of your gift to him will be swiftly redirected to the taxman. At the present time both taxes are charged at 40 per cent so he would have something left – but what if the rates go up?

This is such an important point that you should remember it at all times when thinking about inheritance tax planning and make sure that your professional adviser does not overlook it either.

## Cohabitees

One of the best known exemptions from inheritance tax is the exemption for gifts between husbands and wives and it is for this reason that many wills are prepared on the basis that each spouse leaves everything to the other. With one exception this is a very sensible arrangement. The deceased spouse could have, or should have, arranged to pass £118,000 of his estate to his children (or perhaps in trust for them so that they cannot actually get their hands on the money) because the first £118,000 is tax free anyway. If you leave everything to the surviving spouse you waste this £118,000 tax free band and sooner or later on the death of the surviving spouse, they will have an extra £118,000 to pay tax on. This wasting of the nil rate band on the first death is very expensive (it is worth £47,000) and steps should be taken to make the most of it.

There is an increasing number of people who choose to share their lives without being joined in the honourable estate of holy matrimony. If you are in this situation a really serious problem looms, because on a death any assets passing to the surviving partner do not qualify for any Inheritance Tax exemption at all. This can be absolutely catastrophic. Let us assume that a couple live in a house worth £350,000 with a mortgage of £75,000, the property being owned by the male partner. It is common practice for a life assurance policy to be taken out so that on death the mortgage is paid off. That is a wise precaution because it protects the survivor from being saddled with the mortgage without necessarily having the income with which to meet it. However, that does not solve the Inheritance Tax problem because if the house passes to the survivor, she is lumbered with the inheritance tax liability which just on the value of the house alone (ignoring any other assets which may exist) would be £85,000. (Naturally the figures could be much higher.) How on earth is she going to pay the tax? She could sell the house and move to a smaller house which would probably be exactly what the couple did not intend to happen; alternatively she could borrow the necessary money to pay the Inheritance Tax but this could be an overwhelming financial burden.

This problem can be reduced by arranging to hold the property in joint names so that on a death only half of the property passing to the survivor is chargeable. However, this will probably still not be enough to prevent all the unpleasant consequences. The best way is probably to ensure that both partners lives are adequately insured, so that on the death of one the other becomes entitled to the policy's proceeds which will be sufficient to meet the tax. This does not save any tax but it does provide the money with which to pay it. The third alternative is of course for them to get married but this may well be regarded as taking tax avoidance to rather extreme lengths.

## Repayment Supplement

There is one way in which you can get the better of the tax man and which is thought by many people to be retribution for all the trials and tribulations which they are caused by the Inland Revenue. In chapter 10 it was explained that repayment supplement (that is interest paid to you by the Inland Revenue in respect of overpaid tax) can be generated in connection with income tax. It is much easier to earn supplement from overpaid inheritance tax. It puts the tax man into a real frenzy but you may think it is worth it.

If you make a chargeable transfer (it must be a chargeable transfer – a P.E.T. will not do) such as a transfer into a discretionary settlement, you have a duty to notify the capital taxes office of the transfer and to pay the tax. However, for some reason the rules provide that the notification of such a transfer has to be made within six months, whereas the tax is payable within three months of the transfer. What this means in practice is that you will probably send in your form detailing the transfer with the tax within the three-month period – but this fails to take advantage of a real opportunity to make some money. If your chargeable transfer gives rise to tax of, say, £1,000 and you decide to pay £21,000 on the due date, the tax man will have no means of finding out that you have overpaid tax by £21,000 for at least three months when you send in the return form. In many cases you will not actually know what the liability is because it will depend on values to be negotiated so you would be wise to err on the side of caution and pay the maximum possible amount. It will naturally take him some time to look at the form, decide what to do and to get round to authorising the repayment – possibly another two months or longer depending upon the time of year, so you may therefore have £20,000 invested with the Inland Revenue for five months or more at a competitive rate, but entirely tax free. At the time of writing the rate of repayment supplement on overpaid inheritance tax is 11 per cent per annum tax free which to a 40 per cent taxpayer is worth over 18 per cent per annum so you can really score.

If you feel really adventurous you could keep depositing £20,000 with the capital taxes offices every few months on the basis that you might have made a chargeable transfer but you will let them know later. However, this is going a bit far. The Inland Revenue argue, possibly rightly, that unless there is an actual tax liability, it is not possible to say that you have overpaid tax; all you have done is to pay some money by mistake and that does not qualify for repayment supplement. Whatever you think of the argument this course of action is not recommended because the Inland Revenue certainly will not pay any supplement and you will be out of your money for some time. However, provided you have a real liability, or create one as part of your tax planning arrangements, it is quite possible for you to earn more than enough repayment supplement to cover the whole of the tax and this can be a deeply satisfying achievement.

*Chapter Sixteen*

# DEALING WITH THE SHARES VALUATION DIVISION

# SHARES VALUATION

The Shares Valuation Division of the Inland Revenue is a specialist office which deals primarily with the valuation of shares in private companies for tax purposes. It is independent of any other tax office and cases are referred to the Shares Valuation Division by Inspectors of Taxes whenever an opinion of the value of a private company's shares is needed. Negotiations with the Shares Valuation Division are entirely different from any other negotiations with the Inland Revenue mainly because of this independence; the man at the SVD has no particular interest in the outcome of the negotiations – he is expressing an independent view and when the value is agreed he simply reports it to the relevant tax office who will use the value as appropriate. There may be no tax involved at all – for example it may be a valuation for Capital Gains Tax purposes where the capital gain has been held over or covered by a relief, or the value transferred may be below the various limits at which tax is chargeable. On the other hand there may be a mountain of tax to be paid and each 10p on (or off) the share value may mean big money to the taxpayer.

In many cases the man at the SVD will not know the implications of the value of the shares with which he is faced but you cannot rely on it. All too often the stance of the SVD is aggressively in favour of the Inland Revenue and whilst this may be thought to be inevitable, it cannot be a correct stance if they are supposed to be expressing an independent view. Where the taxpayer is professionally advised, the balance is probably about right provided that the professional adviser is experienced in share valuation; but where the taxpayer is on his own he is at a considerable disadvantage – but he is always at a disadvantage when dealing with the Inland Revenue so perhaps nothing really changes. It is for this reason that share valuations should not be conducted by the uninformed taxpayer – he will be buried in a trice by the experienced valuers in the Shares Valuations Division. Accordingly this chapter is mainly directed to those who have a good understanding of the nature of a share in a company, including professional advisers who are not perhaps particularly experienced in the field.

The involvement of the Shares Valuation Division starts by a referral from another tax office. For example, you send in your tax return which shows that you have given 10 per cent of the shares in your family company to your son. For a number of tax purposes the value of the gift will be important and the SVD will be asked to express their view on the value of the shares so that the tax can be computed. Before 1985 such a gift could give rise to three separate valuations – one for Stamp Duty, one for Capital Gains Tax and another for Capital Transfer Tax. Inevitably, each tax had its own valuation principles and so the value of the shares for the purposes of each tax is different. The abolition of Stamp Duty on gifts in 1985 means that Stamp Duty valuations of shares in private companies are now comparatavely rare and the advent of Inheritance Tax and the concept of potentially exempt transfers means that values for Inheritance Tax purposes are now less often required – at least in respect of life time transfers. Until recently, Capital Gains Tax hold over relief was freely available in respect of all types of gift so the value at the date of the actual gift was irrelevant for all practical purposes. Hold over relief enables the donor to escape a charge to Capital Gains Tax on his gift (which would otherwise be treated for Capital Gains Tax purposes as a disposal at market value and taxed accordingly) by claiming that the capital gain be 'held over' until such time as the donee himself disposes of the asset. Now that hold over relief has been restricted to certain limited circumstances, Capital Gains Tax will arise more often on a gift and the need for negotiations to take place with the Shares Valuation Division will therefore tend to increase.

It may be thought to be an advantage to avoid having to nego- tiate share values in respect of a particular transaction but this is not always the case. The value at the date of disposal is bound to have a significance at some stage and it is useful to have it agreed, whether you want a low or high valuation. Further- more, not knowing the value of the gifts that you have made gives rise to an undesirable degree of uncertainty. For Capital Gains Tax purposes it is often possible to insist that the shares be properly valued because, for example, it is the gain which is held over by a hold over relief claim and this claim cannot be made until the gain is established – and this means that the shares must be valued. If for some reason the Shares Valuation Division are reluctant to agree a value on these grounds, you can always defer submitting your claim for relief until such time as the value is agreed – you have six years in which to make most claims. All this gives you an enormous advantage in your negotiations with the Shares Valuation Division.

Essentially, the man at the SVD wants to reach agreement on a sensible value for your company shares. He may or may not be aware of the precise tax implications but he would normally conclude from his knowledge of the transactions concerning the shares that some tax liability is going to be involved. He can therefore deduce that his efforts in agreeing to a high value will probably be rewarded by the Inland Revenue being able to charge more tax. However, if you mention in passing (you need to mention it a few times in passing just so that he does not forget) that there is no tax at stake because a hold over relief claim is going to be made, his work will be deprived of any real purpose. He has his professional pride of course, and a public duty to perform but he can perhaps be forgiven if he pays less attention to your valuation than the many others on his plate where there is some real tax involved, and he is therefore prepared to accept your comparatavely low valuation somewhat more readily. You therefore have a real opportunity here to agree a favourable valuation.

If there is no tax involved you may wonder where the advantage lies. It lies in establishing the value for the share transfer in question so that it can be used as a basis for subsequent transfers of shares in the same company by the same or other shareholders. Although no two shareholdings will be worth the same because the circumstances of the buyer and the seller will be different, it is reasonable enough (and common practice) for sensibly agreed values to be used as the basis for subsequent transfers. So having made a gift of shares of say 10 per cent to your son, and held the gain over, you now have a benchmark to be used for other transfers. This would of course only really apply for Capital Gains Tax. but it is not unusual for the same value to be used for Inheritance Tax purposes as well, unless the disposal causes the donor's shareholding to cross an important percentage threshold – for example giving away a handful of shares which deprives the donor of control of the company (this is explained in more detail later).

Having established a value you are now able to make further transfers of the company's shares with a fairly accurate idea of what the tax consequences would be. This is particularly important for Inheritance Tax purposes because the current stance of the Shares Valuation Division is that they will not enter into correspondence regardings share values if it is clear that no tax will be payable. This is much more significant than it would first appear because what it means is that if you are proposing to give away any shares in the family trading company, the gift has to be worth £250,000 before the Shares Valuation Division will bother with valuing the gift for Inheritance Tax purposes. By way of explanation this £250,000 figure is found as under:

| | |
|---|---|
| Value of Shares | £250,000 |
| Business Relief at 50% | £125,000 |
| | £125,000 |
| Less Annual Exemptions (this year and last year) | £  6,000 |
| | £119,000 |
| Inheritance Tax Nil Rate Band | £118,000 |
| Chargeable Transfer | £  1,000 |

Furthermore, the gift has to be a *chargeable* transfer – a potentially exempt transfer will not do. The most usual chargeable transfer is a transfer to a discretionary settlement (see page 184) andd there will not be too many people who are prepared to put £250,000 worth of their company's shares into a discretionary trust just to establish a share value. You may have already secured a value for Capital Gains Tax purposes and hope that it can be used as an indication of the Inheritance Tax value but you do need to take care over concepts such as related property and the loss to the donor principle (explained further below), because these can seriously upset the value for Inheritance Tax purposes on which you may be basing your thinking.

Two examples can perhaps be given to illustrate how important it can be to obtain a favourable valuation in the manner outlined above. For example, you may have a successful family company and would like to arrange for some of your shares to be held by an offshore trust (now is not the time nor the place to explain the advantages of offshore trusts – suffice it to say that they can be highly advantageous in terms of Capital Gains

Tax planning – although they are a complete waste of time if you are trying to save income tax). A gift to an offshore trust is a disposal for Capital Gains Tax on which tax is payable as if you had sold the shares for market value – no hold over relief is available on such a transfer because the donee is not resident. If you give the shares to overseas trustees without knowing the value you will create a Capital Gains Tax liability but you have no idea what the amount will be. Nobody is likely to want to do that. However, if you have already made a small gift of shares and established a value, you have a good idea what the value of your gift into the offshore trust will be and can plan accordingly.

It is possible to be a good deal more subtle than this. If you make a transfer to a UK settlement you can hold over the gain and this gives you the opportunity to make a Capital Gains Tax disposal to the desired type of trust without creating any unnecessary tax. If you are happy with the value which is ultimately agreed with the SVD you can then export the settlement by appointing non-resident trustees. (This is a complex procedure which cannot possibly be undertaken without professional help.) Without going into all the technicalities, at the date of export the held-over gain, that is the gain which was previously deferred on the original transfer to the trustees, immediately becomes chargeable. You know what the gain is because the value has been agreed and you therefore know exactly what your tax liability will be if you export the settlement. If you were not happy with the share valuation which was agreed at the time you may choose not to export the settlement but you have a choice and you know exactly the consequences of each course of action.

The second illustration concerns Inheritance Tax. If you transfer shares in your company to a discretionary trust, that is a chargeable transfer which needs to be valued for Inheritance Tax purposes. However, as explained in Chapter 15, where the SVD are satisfied that no tax will actually become payable, they will decline to express a view concerning the value. However, it is possible to extract from them an assurance that the share value does not exceed a certain figure and although this is not as firm as an agreed valuation, there is no reason why it cannot be relied on. The advantage here is that the shares can be distributed within a period of ten years from the discretionary trust without any Inheritance Tax liability arising by virtue of the earlier assurance.

These examples illustrate how useful it can be to take advantage of the SVD's unwillingness to spend time valuing shares on transactions which give rise to no immediate tax liability, but will provide you with a long term advantage.

### Different Share Holdings

Whenever you are faced with valuing shares you must look at the holding to be valued and appreciate that different holdings will always have different values. For example, a 51 per cent holding is obviously worth a good deal more than a 49 per cent holding because having 51 per cent gives control of the company and a 49 per cent holding does not. There are many other key percentages to be considered and you will always need to keep in mind the particular attributes of specific percentage holdings. Every ounce of ammunition is needed when negotiating with the SVD and the following might be useful:

90 per cent: a 90 per cent holding gives you the power in certain circumstances to acquire the rest of the shares whether the other shareholders want to sell to you or not. This is not an easy procedure but it can be done and therefore enhances the value of a 90 per cent holding compared with a 89 per cent holding. This is a useful point to bring out if you are seeking to agree a high valuation. If you are seeking a low valuation it is clearly something to be ignored and you should make reference to the fact that a 10 per cent shareholder has a considerable nuisance value and can apply to the court for protection if he feels his rights are being infringed. This is clearly a devaluing influence which may be useful.

75 per cent: this holding gives you the power to pass a special resolution which is needed to take all the important decisions regarding a company's affairs – and perhaps most importantly the power to wind the company up and to distribute the company's assets to its shareholders. Unless you have 75 per cent it is probably idle to value the company on the basis that it could be wound up and there are good grounds to resist an assets basis valuation at all – provided of course that it is to your advantage to do so.

51 per cent: this holding gives you control of the company and enables you to pass an ordinary resolution which can remove directors at the Annual General Meeting and generally do all the other administrative things a company wants to do – but you cannot wind the company up with this level of shareholding. It is obviously valuable – much more valuable than not being in control, but you should not ignore the fact that there are other 49 per cent shareholders who can be extremely influential in the company's affairs.

Generally speaking shareholdings in excess of 50 per cent will be valued on what is known as a discounted assets basis – that is to say the value of the assets of the company less a discount for unmarketability and the trouble and risk of getting the assets out of the company. These discounts are highly negotiable and although there are some percentages often quoted for discounts on various holdings, these seem to be honoured more in the breach than in the observance. In any event you should be aware of two decided cases which will be of immense help in negotiating a much lower value than a straight assets basis. The first is the case of Battle v. IRC in which even a holding of 98 per cent in a company which was all ready to be liquidated was still worth a discount of 2.5 per cent on net assets. Just think what you can do with a slightly smaller holding in a company which is not ready to be liquidated – or indeed in a trading company which is not easily wound up without considerable stock losses, bad debts, etc. This is an extremely valuable case which you should have in your armoury when seeking a lower valuation. The other relevant case is re Courthope in which the court recognized that any purchaser of a company who wants to get his hands on the company's assets will not do it for nothing. He will want to take into account all the costs and liabilities of getting hold of the assets (so you need to think about, and work out, all the likely fees, costs, liquidator's charges, realization expenses etc. including tax) and furthermore the purchaser will still want to make a profit – in the case of Courthope the court suggested that this profit should be 50 per cent so even in the clearest case on an assets basis valuation it is possible to argue very substantial reductions from the value of the net asset on a straight arithmetical proportion.

Below 50 per cent and you move into what is known as the yield basis of valuation; you cannot pass any kind of resolution on your own and you are therefore not able to get your hands on any of the assets – you are at the mercy of the controlling shareholder if there is one. Even if there is not a controlling shareholder you still cannot get your way without finding somebody else to agree with you and that is a matter of speculation which has no place in share valuation.

26 per cent: in terms of shareholder power, there is not much difference between a 49 per cent shareholding and a 26 per cent shareholding – both can block a special resolution but little else. The Shares Valuation Division tend to ascribe value to the fact that a special resolution can be blocked by such shareholdings and they should be pressed to give reasons why this is thought to be valuable. You may have to concede a small element of value for this point, but not very much.

Under 25 per cent: at this level you are pretty much on your own and are clearly at the mercy of the other shareholders. You could try to sell your shares but might have great difficulty doing so because all a purchaser can do is hope to receive a dividend, or hope that the company will be wound up or sold so that he can get some part of the assets. Neither possibility can be taken seriously into account and such small holdings must always be valued very poorly. Any attempt by the SVD to put anything other than a comparatively nominal value on the shares should be resisted.

Minority shareholders are invariably valued on the yield basis – that is to say on the basis of the earnings and dividends of the company. It is sometimes thought to be the amount of dividends you receive from the company but that is a mistaken view. The yield on shares for this purpose should be based on the dividends which the company could pay if it wanted to. A 20 per cent shareholding in a company making £1 million profits per year is not worthless just because it has never paid a dividend – nor is it worth a fortune because a company pays an enormous dividend in one year. In some circumstances even a 20 per cent shareholder can insist on a dividend being paid, although this is not an aspect you would wish to bring out if you are seeking a low valuation – but it is very useful if you would like a high value. You need to look at the profits available for distribution and consider the level of dividend which could regularly be paid by the company, taking into account appropriate dividend cover, the resources available to the company and the need for investment in new plant and other commitments. Always remember that it is the maintainable dividend that matters, not a special dividend paid because of some special circumstances in a particular year. You need to calculate the amount of dividend which the company could have paid in the last few years bearing in mind the above consideration and whether this is likely to continue; this will be the maintainable dividend to be used as the determinant of the share price. But again, do not allow the SVD to get carried away with this aspect – the company may have no money, it may have very high stocks and debtors and may not sensibly be able to pay a regular dividend. Consider also whether a regular dividend might cause the company to become insolvent; if any possibility of this can be put forward there may be no maintainable dividend and the value of the shares would therefore be extremely low.

With all the above it is necessary to have up-to-date information at the date of the valuation but you must only have regard to the information which is actually available at that date or could reasonably have been made available to a prospective purchaser. The purchaser of a 90 per cent holding would obviously be given access to all the company's books and records and would no doubt send in a team of accountants to pore over the books but a 25 per cent shareholder would not be given such information. All he would have is the published information if anything at all. He may not be able to get hold of anything more than what is available at Companies House and even if the company is late in filing its accounts there is not much that a purchaser of a 25 per cent shareholding can do about it. You should always make quite sure that you know exactly what information was available at the date of the valuation and exclude all other information from your consideration. Hindsight is absolutely prohibited and tends to be most damaging if you are seeking a low valuation. Values tend to go up (presumably that is why the shares were given away in the first place) so if you use hindsight for example by looking at subsequent accounts you will have the benefit of seeing how the company has performed in the period since the shares were transferred. This is not information available at the date of the transfer and it is wholly wrong to use it because at the date of the valuation one has to take into account all the risks and uncertainties inherent in such a shareholding. If the valuation date is 1 January 1990 and the accounts for the year ended 30 June 1989 are not available at that date, they should not be used for the purposes of a minority share valuation. The

SVD like to see subsequent years' accounts and such requests should always be denied – but accompanied by a full and reasoned explanation.

## Different Bases of Valuation

Negotiations with the Shares Valuation Division are always undertaken for a specific purpose – that is to obtain a valuation of the shares which suits your circumstances; usually that is the lowest possible valuation but sometimes you want a high valuation – that possibility is dealt with later. To achieve a low valuation you need to have regard to all the points made earlier, but you must also appreciate the specific statutory valation rules for the particular tax as they may seriously affect the valuation principles. You also need a good deal of inspiration.

It is not appropriate to go into detail here but you must be aware of the different bases of valuation for Capital Gains Tax and Inheritance Tax. For Capital Gains Tax the rule is that the parcel of shares must be valued at market value which is the price at which they might reasonably be expected to fetch on a sale on the open market, but in estimating this value no reduction is allowed for the assumption that the whole of the shares would be placed on the market at the same time. For Capital Gains Tax purposes you value the parcel of shares actually given away – it is irrelevant how valuable they are to the purchaser or how valuable they were to you. If you give away 2 per cent of your 51 per cent holding you have deprived yourself of an enormous amount of value but the subject matter of the gift is still only a holding of 2 per cent of the shares, it is a parcel of 2 per cent which has to be valued.

For Inheritance Tax purposes the position is entirely different; whilst the basic market value rule is the same, you also have to consider the loss to the donor. If you are giving away 2 per cent of the shares in your company and this will reduce your shareholding from 51 per cent to 49 per cent, the value of the shares transferred will be the difference between a 51 per cent holding which gives control and a 49 per cent holding which does not. This will be an enormous difference and it will be many times the the value of the simple 2 per cent holding. There is a further special provision for Inheritance Tax which is the concept of 'related property'. What this means is that you have to value the shares of a husband as part of the combined holding of himself and his wife. Therefore if a husband and a wife each have a 30 per cent shareholding you must not value any transfer of the husband's shares as a minority holding but as a proportion of a 60 per cent holding – which will obviously be valued much more highly as a majority holding. Accordingly if the husband gives away 15 per cent out of his holding this will be valued as the difference between a 60 per cent holding and a 45 per cent holding. This difference, which will be the measure of the gift for Inheritance Tax purposes, will be much larger than you may imagine.

The importance of these two concepts cannot be emphasized too highly as they must be taken into account in all Inheritance Tax valuations.

With all share valuations it is important to bear in mind that the valuation is entirely artificial and based on a hypothetical sale. What is equally important is to recognize the attributes of the assumed prospective purchaser who is always regarded as a prudent man of business. You should therefore be alert to all suggestions by the SVD which border on speculation. A prudent man of business does not engage in speculation and this should be drawn to the attention of the SVD at every available opportunity.

*Inspiration*

The trouble with share valuations is that they require a good understanding of company accounts because it is the company accounts which will always be the primary information on which the valuation is based. If you cannot interpret company accounts you have a real problem and you are not going to have a lot of success with the SVD, who are trained to do so. However, leaving that particular difficulty aside, having obtained all the relevant information available at the date of the valuation you should scrutinize earlier accounts of the company; you need to sit and stare at them for a very long time and think of every conceivable reason why the company is worth very little. Your approach may vary depending upon whether you are considering a minority or majority holding but essentially the task is the same. If you are looking at the assets of the company you should consider the following points:

a) The type of assets possessed by the company and what would happen if they were sold. Do they have any real saleable value or are they just motor vehicles and plant which would have very little scrap or secondhand value? If so they need to be discounted very heavily.

b) How much of the company's current assets are represented by stock, work in progress and debtors? Stock tends to be shown at cost but it is only of any real value when it is sold. Until that time there is a lot of value tied up in the stock, all of which may not be able to be recovered if it had to be sold quickly. Work in progress is in the same broad category. Partially completed work is of very little value and the figure shown in the accounts for work in progress will be based on the assumption that the company will be continuing as a going concern. If there is doubt whether the company would continue as a going concern the work in progress must be discounted extremely heavily. Similarly, when a business comes to an end the debtors become extremely difficult to collect because there is no incentive for the company's debtors to make payment – they have lost a customer and they no longer have to maintain a good business relationship. Accordingly the incidence of bad debts increases dramatically.

c) The extent of the company's borrowings and creditors need to be examined. If the creditors cannot all be paid unless the company collects it debts and sells some more of its products one can construct a very unfavourable picture. Continuing support from the company's bankers may be required and if this were to be withdrawn (for example if the company hit a period of adverse trading) this could have an extremely serious effect on the company's future. Can it be said that the company is perilously close to being insolvent? If such an argument can be put forward it has the most enormously depressing effect on the value of the company's shares.

d) Have any of the company's assets been revalued and if so has the deferred taxation been fully taken into account – that is the tax which would arise on the revaluation if the assets were to be sold on the revalued figure? This is not something which any prudent man of business could possibly overlook although the SVD like to try to do so.

e) Are the company's assets growing in value? If not you can predict a general decline in the asset backing for your shares and the company may be heading for disaster. A prospective purchaser of the shares would be locked in and could do little but watch the value of his investment decline.

f) Can you point to any reason why the company can be said to be poorly managed? The assets may be old (look at the notes to the accounts to see whether there are regular additions to plant and machinery); if not there may be heavy expenditure required in the near future to restore these old assets and this may not be readily apparent from the figures. Are the guarantees or contingent liabilities shown in the notes to the accounts? These could crystallize and wipe out the value of the company's shares. Are the directors interested in contracts with the company? If so this might indicate that they have outside interests which might cause the management of the company to go away unexpectedly and leave the company to its own devices.

You can go on for ever like this and the more ideas you can come up with the more you can put forward as reasons why a prudent prospective purchaser would be extremely nervous about investing his money in this company. No prudent man of business would think of investing good money (or at least not much of it) in buying shares in a company afflicted by any of the problems mentioned above.

If you are looking at the shares on a dividend yield basis you might consider:

a) Looking at the pattern of profit growth over a number of years, comparing it with the Retail Price Index and calculating the real growth. You could go on to compare this with the statistics for the industry as a whole. You may well find that the company is lagging behind the industry or possibly going backwards. On this basis profits are almost certain to decline and the whole future of the company would be at risk, thereby depressing the value of the company's shares still further.

b) Looking at the exceptional items shown in the accounts; there may have been capital gains which have bolstered up the profits for some years – exclude them and do your calculations again. Capital gains are generally not recurring items and the future of the company must depend upon its sound trading operations – not windfall gains. A prudent prospective purchaser is not interested in windfall gains – they are speculative good fortune and he must be looking for soundness.

c) Again you must look for reasons why the company can be thought of as being poorly managed – a high debtors' ratio might indicate a poor performance in collecting debts which may mask possible bad debts in the future. Consideration of the gross profit percentage is most important; is it stable and how does it compare with the industry norm? If it is higher than the industry norm you can say the company is at high risk, charging excessive prices which cannot last, indicating that a decline is likely; if the gross profit percentage is lower than the industry norm the company is clearly under-performing and a decline in the company's fortunes is again likely.

All these things require a good deal of attention and inspiration but the more you think the more inspiration you will come up with about why the company is probably on the rocks and not able to support anything other than a purely nominal valuation. After all this you must be prepared to present these points persuasively to the Shares Valuation Division. They will inevitably argue but you can reasonably point out that their job is not to resist your arguments; their job is to take a balanced view about the proper value to be ascribed to the shares and they cannot just dismiss the points you put forward if they are soundly based. If the SVD concentrate only on the good points supporting a high value and overlook the areas of risk and uncertainty they are not approaching the matter properly and you should say so.

## P. E. Ratios

It is not unusual for the SVD to quote Price/Earnings ratios to arrive at a value of shares in a private company. They do not do this to confuse (although that is often the effect) but simply to draw a comparison between a private company where there is no published market price and a public company where they are selling prices published every day in the Financial Times. They are extremely keen on P.E. ratios and you must be equally keen to reject any such comparison. There is a world of difference between a private company and a public company and any such comparison is wholly false – even where the private company is so large that it could sensibly seek a Stock Exchange quotation it must be pointed out that it is not a quoted company and the comparison is at best weak and at worse grossly misleading.

A P.E. ratio is nothing more than an index figure whereby the company's total value can be computed as a multiple of its current earnings. For example if a company makes £100,000 profit after tax this year and the average P. E. ratio for the quoted companies in the same industry is 10, the value would be 10 times the profits which is £1 million for the whole of the company's shares. A little thought reveals that this is a hopeless conclusion, because P.E. ratios change every day with movements in the share prices on the Stock Exchange. Furthermore the average P.E. ratios quoted are made up from very large companies all of which are probably much larger than your company. Even then, the average P. E. ratio will be made up of some companies with a P.E. ratio of say 4 and others with a P.E. ratio of say 18 so this would give a huge variation in the possible value of any company, vitiating the entire exercise. In any event the P.E. ratio is based on the whole of the company's shares and not on a smaller shareholding.

All this shows that a comparison with quoted P.E. ratios is an almost worthless exercise in a private company's share valuation and you should never allow yourself to be sucked into such a discussion. It will rarely do you any good because quoted share prices of public companies will almost always be much higher than would be appropriate for a private company – not least because people can buy and sell quoted shares quickly and easily and this enhances the available market and keeps the price high. Once you are in a private company you are stuck unless and until somebody will buy your shares. The answer to these profound differences is definitely not to take a P. E. ratio and then reduce it by some percentage. This just makes further nonsense of an already nonsensical calculation.

Just think – if you have 25 per cent of the shares in a private company and you want to sell, who on earth would you get to buy the shares from you? Keep this in mind and then you will always be quite clear how difficult it is to sell and why you can and ought to negotiate a low value with the SVD.

The above explains some of the ways in which you can negotiate with the SVD to keep the valuation of your company's shares to a minimum. It will involve lengthy and detailed correspondence. You should not be afraid of writing extremely long letters to the SVD provided of course that that they are sensible and relevant. It will show that you have understood the points involved and have looked at the matters in detail. Do not leave anything out and do not bother about being brief with your arguments. It is much better that you make your points twice then risk a good point being missed by the taxman. Some people like to feed the arguments to the SVD one at a time so that they pick off each of the SVD arguments one by one but I do not greatly favour this approach. It can be useful if you are trying to lead the SVD along a line of argument where you have the ability to deliver a *coup de grace* – but such circumstances are rare and you have to be very knowledgeable indeed to be able to do so. In the vast majority of cases it is preferable to give the SVD the whole load at once so that the taxman gets an immediate impression that the company is worthless; he may later take another view but you start off the initiative. Leave him on his own at the beginning so that he comes to the view that the company is valuable and you will have an uphill struggle dispelling his first impressions.

Neither should you be afraid of receiving long letters from the SVD – the more they say the more there is for you to argue with and you should do so. You can always find lots of ammunition in any long letter from the SVD that indicates for example that they are concentrating only on areas favourable to their point of view, or not taking full account of your arguments, or indeed bringing in points which are irrelevant. When you receive such a letter from the SVD you should *immediately*, while all the points are fresh in your mind, go through the letter in great detail and note carefully all the points with which you disagree and all the underlying reasoning. If necessary draft your full reply – but do not send it. Leave it for a few months until the taxman has forgotten all about the case and then send it to him. He will then read your letter afresh without a full familiarity with all his previous arguments and if your letter is persuasive he is more likely to be favourably disposed towards your arguments.

If you are lucky he will have been transferred or promoted or the case will have been re-allocated to another person and you will have a new correspondent who is much less familiar with the case. This may not always be an improvement but he will certainly be less well placed to argue with your points until he has got to grips with the case.

Always end your letter with a proposition that he can agree with, if he wants to; for example a recapitulation of what your value is and why it should be accepted, or possibly a compromise offer so that he will have the immediate opportunity to agree and settle the case if your proposals sound reasonable (and after all he will be reasonably keen to settle the case – it is not in his interest to drag the matter out). He will be keenly aware after reading your second or third extremely long letter that if he continues to disagree he is going to get another six pages of argument and this might just encourage him to agree.

# CONCLUSION

The aim of this book has been to inform and to guide those who are neither expert nor experienced in the subject so that trouble with the taxman can be avoided – or at least seen on the horizon in time for something to be done to limit the damage. It is a question of knowing your opponent and the forces he has at his disposal – and his personality may be just as important as his artillery.

It should always be remembered that being right is never enough when dealing with the taxman – you have to prove that you are right and you should never underestimate his awesome power. The trick is to encourage him not to use all his power but to come to a conclusion which is fair and reasonable.

Principles are important, and they should be maintained by both you and the Inland Revenue at all times; by sticking to your principles you can insist that he does likewise. How you deal with the taxman may well determine how he approaches your affairs. It is possible to be both firm and flexible (rather like the head of one of our largest companies who was recently described as being both 'blunt' and 'sharp') and this, combined with unfailing courtesy, will put you in the best possible position with the Inland Revenue during good times and bad. Sometime, somehow, something will go wrong and you will need every ounce of imagination and diplomacy (and possibly inspiration derived from this book) to keep you out of difficulty.